BTL

LIFE LESSONS FROM
REMARKABLE
WOMEN

LIFE LESSONS FROM
REMARKABLE
WOMEN

Tales of triumph,
failure & learning
to love yourself

PENGUIN LIFE

AN IMPRINT OF

PENGUIN BOOKS

PENGUIN LIFE

UK | USA | Canada | Ireland | Australia
India | New Zealand | South Africa

Penguin Life is part of the Penguin Random House
group of companies whose addresses can be found at
global.penguinrandomhouse.com.

First published 2018
001

Copyright © Shortlist Media Limited, 2018

The moral right of the copyright holders has been asserted

Designed by Hampton Associates
Printed in Italy by L.E.G.O. S.p.A

A CIP catalogue record for this book is available from the British Library

ISBN: 978-0-241-32282-6

When *Stylist* launched in October 2009, we had a very specific agenda in mind: to create a thought-provoking, empowering and overtly feminist media brand that would only raise women up as opposed to tear them down.

Staying true to our manifesto meant sticking to a few rules: diets – and any other form of negative body scrutiny – were strictly off limits; scurrilous gossip and conjecture were to be avoided at all costs; and lastly, we would only ever seek out interviews with informed, talented and inspirational women.

And for the majority of the past decade we have had countless of those women on our pages: from Hillary Clinton and Nigella Lawson, to Jessica Ennis and Sheryl Sandberg and beyond – all sharing their wisdom and experience with the *Stylist* audience.

It was the desire to harness this wisdom which in 2014 saw us launch our hugely successful Life Lessons franchise: a series of events designed to give the women we respect and admire a platform to share their number one 'life lesson' in a succinct fifteen-minute talk. Passing on the words of wisdom they've used to steer their own lives and decisions to women everywhere in a wonderfully digestible way.

But if it's worth saying out loud, then it's most definitely worth writing down. And so here we are with our very first Life Lessons book: an anthology of essays from twenty-five inspirational women that includes everyone from Olympic boxing champion Nicola Adams OBE to self-made businesswoman Bobbi Brown and foreign correspondent Christina Lamb OBE. Their life lessons are varied; some endearing and bittersweet, others brimming with confidence and empowerment. But all are must-read and enriching – sentiments and learnings to return to again and again.

Lisa Smosarski, Editor-in-Chief, *Stylist*

CONTENTS

LIFE LESSONS

LISA SMOSARSKI

LIFE LESSON NO.1
WHY HAVING IT
ALL IS A MYTH

The clock at the corner of my screen flashed to 17:01 and I scanned the office. The designers were animatedly brainstorming, the editors scratched away at a tower of proofs while the writers tapped feverishly on their keyboards, all working as fast as they could to hit deadline. Me? I was picking up my handbag and trying to sidle out of the room, desperate not to be noticed.

'See you tomorrow,' I whispered as I slipped out the door. I knew half the team were going to be sat there for another three or four hours, probably eating dinner at their desks. And where was I going? Home, that was where, to the seven-month-old baby I'd left for the first time that morning.

As I faced the unfamiliar 5 p.m. scrum on the packed tube train I was racked with guilt. Not for my baby, that was something I'd expected, planned and steeled myself for. No, it was for the colleagues I'd left at their desks. I had never been scared to put the hours in. In fact, I'd never not been the last person in the office. And now what had I done? Abandoned them, that's what. I really hadn't anticipated just how hard that was going to be.

I spent the next few years trying to make it work. I'd leave home at 7.20 a.m. and start sending emails on the bus, head to the office to a day packed with relentless meetings, run – often late – for nursery pick up, bathe my son, then pick up my phone, laptop or pile of proofs and carry on. I'd work antisocially, sending emails at 6 a.m. or 11 p.m. that people then felt obliged to reply to. Cue more guilt. Looking back I can acknowledge that was my way of trying to avoid invisibility, but by trying to prove I was putting in the hours I was working longer – and harder – than ever before.

So this was having it all then, was it? The concept I'd grown up just accepting would be mine. Feeling guilty at home. Guilty at work. And completely bloody exhausted.

Our feminist foremothers had spent years fighting for this, millions of books had been sold on the topic, so why was I finding it so tough? I'm not the first woman in the world to have a career and a baby, after all. And more importantly, was this the having it all I'd been working so hard for?

The more I danced this tango the more I questioned it. Because who – name me just one person, man or woman – has it 'all'? When you stop and think about it, that's a pretty ridiculous notion. Greedy even. Who needs it all? There's only twenty-four hours in a day and it's compulsory for you to sleep for some of them. At least for a bit.

Of course the idea of having it all was born from the philosophy that women could – and should – be entitled to choose a family and a career. Just like men. That choosing a family didn't mean having to stay home. Or by choosing a career you were destined for a life without children or a partner. It was an important part of a feminist fight by brave and resilient women – and, don't get me wrong, one which I will be eternally grateful for. I wouldn't be me without my career. Or my family for that matter.

But that concept has evolved and mutated. It's hard to pinpoint the exact beginnings of our current 'having it all' – a shorthand for doing everything in life brilliantly – and, most importantly, without guilt. But the launch of a 1982 book by the legendary editor of US *Cosmopolitan* Helen Gurley Brown, entitled *Having It All: Love, Success, Sex, Money, Even If You're*

Starting With Nothing, has got to be fairly important. The title of that book created a global myth that as women we could – and should – be living every part of our lives to the full. Or we were somehow failing miserably. Unlike our male peers who were still carrying on as before, having, but not *doing*, both. It made women feel they were lacking if they wanted to stay home with their families. And vice versa – what is wrong with wanting to forgo family for a career? 'Having it all' came to stand for the life goals for a new wave of feminists – not just a quest to be equal with men, but to do it better somehow. It was recently revealed that Gurley Brown had never liked the title of the book or the tone it set, but the publishers had pushed it through. How I wish Gurley Brown had won that battle.

Before I knew it, I was unwittingly perpetuating the myth too. As editor-in-chief of *Stylist* I became known as a career woman with kids, often asked to take a seat on panels for working women on how to 'juggle' (*gag*, a hideous genderized word . . . but that's a whole other essay) to explain my secrets to doing it all. The rooms were always full because it turns out, for most women (read humans), it's quite a big ask. Guests were expectant that some life-changing tip was about to be revealed that would make this expectation an easy reality. But I didn't have any advice. How would I know? I felt guilty all the time. I missed important work dinners and bring-your-parent-to-nursery days. I would turn up to drinks with friends late. And my husband? Well if we got to have dinner that was a novelty. And I was working. All. The. Time. I would peer at my tiny phone screen for hours each day. Getting home in the evening, the point at which I'd be swapping from my very literal editor's heels to comfy flats, I'd feel blurry and jittery, bogged in a cortisol haze. I didn't feel good.

But the questions continued. 'How on earth do you do it?' people would ask expectantly. 'I don't,' I'd reply flatly. And it was that question which finally made me accept my truth.

'I can't do it all. And . . . (whisper it) . . . neither can you.'

Yes, I felt like a traitor to the cause, the archetypal Bad Feminist, but this admission felt good. Because it was the first time I'd admitted it to myself too, that I *couldn't* do it all. No one could. And that was never the point anyway. The message just got muddled along the way.

So I'm not saying you shouldn't aspire to have a career and a family. In fact, I'm saying the opposite . . . go for it. You can have both. Because I do. And for that, I think my life is pretty great, stress and angst included. But I just don't think I'll ever have it 'all'. And by that I mean the perfect amount of time at home with my children, a full presence at the school gates and in the office, feeling fulfilled in all my personal ambitions while fulfilling the needs of others. Oh and, you know, hosting fabulous parties, ensuring my kids don't live on fish fingers alone, always having washed and bouncy hair, being up to date on all the books I have piled by my bed while also understanding every intricacy of the Brexit negotiations, ready to discuss passionately with interesting strangers in cool new bars. That 'have it all'. Because I have tried. And failed. And so will everyone else. And that failure steals from all the great stuff we actually *do* have.

Because you can have a hell of a lot. And certainly as much as a man, which is where this all started anyway. But it does involve the dreaded C word . . . compromise. Something our male compadres learned a long time ago. Historically, men worked long days in the office but were often absent at home. That's not the dream. Nor the goal. But it is compromise.

YOU CAN HAVE A HELL OF A LOT AND DO IT AMAZINGLY. YOU JUST CAN'T HAVE IT ALL.

So for me that means being more flexible, letting my priorities fluctuate. I've cancelled a trip to Milan Fashion Week to be with my son for his first day at school. And I would do it again in a flash. But there will be other occasions when I need to sit down and explain why mummy won't be there, that I need to be at work instead. Compromise.

I know I'm lucky to have what I've got. A truly fantastic career, three incredible children, a patient husband and the best of friends. And now I've stopped chasing that elusive 'all' I'm hoping I'll be able to enjoy it too.

Oprah, a woman I rarely quote, but I should because she is a sage of our time, once said, 'You can have it all, just not all at once.' And these are words I can squarely get on board with. Because having it all is really about learning the art of patience. Of finding a way through your busy life to get what YOU want out of it. And not punishing yourself when you have to say, 'I can't do that' – whatever your 'that' might be. So when that clock next hits 17:01 and you really do have to leave, do it with pride. Don't skulk to the door; tap dance, fanfare, own the life you've created. You can have a hell of a lot and do it amazingly. You just can't have it all.

BOBBI BROWN

LIFE LESSON NO.2
THE JOY OF STARTING OVER

**I am someone who likes a challenge. I am
incredibly curious, I like the unknown, and I like
to try new things. I believe in simple solutions,
but I like to challenge myself to identify more
interesting ways to do things. As soon as
something stops being challenging, I like to change
it up. When I do the same thing over and over
again, I stop being inspired and stop producing my
best work.**

That's not to say change is always easy. I think a lot, but often
act without thinking. That was not the case, however, when I
made the decision to leave my namesake brand after almost
twenty-seven years. That was not an instant decision. I didn't
just wake up and say, 'today's the day'. The brand was my baby,
my pride and joy, and who I was. I believed make-up should be
simple and easy to apply. I loved being able to teach women
the simplicity of beauty, but also how to rock a smoky eye or a
bright red lip. I was surrounded by amazing and inspirational
creative teams, who were also my friends. There were so many
reasons I loved my job, until I didn't any more.

Things weren't working for me and I was becoming
increasingly frustrated and aggravated. There was and is a
shift happening, not only at the brand, but in the industry.
At first, I was optimistic (and a bit naive) and thought I
could fix things and make everything better. I was vocal and
honest. I told the truth. I confided in many of my mentors and
confidants, seeking guidance from them. I held the hope that
I could make a difference and turn things around as I had so
many times before in the company's history. I am the kind of
person who likes to forge her own path, and whenever I see
something isn't working, I look for a solution.

There are people who stay in unhappy marriages for way too long. Sometimes for financial reasons, or sometimes it's fear or simply feeling stuck. To stay in a situation that isn't working for you, whether it's a job or a relationship, isn't healthy. Sure, it's risky to upend your life and start over again – but if you don't take a chance then you'll never know.

When I did decide that it was time to leave, I knew instinctively that I'd done the right thing. First I felt relieved, then I was excited about all of the possibilities ahead of me. All the things I didn't have time to do, I could now make time for. I have never been to the Statue of Liberty; I haven't sat in a café with a cappuccino in years; I still want to take hip-hop dance classes, and I really want to be available to do last-minute things with my husband, boys and girlfriends. The world is my oyster.

However, I'd be lying if I told you this has all happened since my departure from the brand. There were a few weeks spent with lawyers and new PR people to handle my announcement and my exit from the company. There were emotions that I wasn't expecting to feel, like anger, sadness and loss. I've learned that these feelings were normal for me to experience. It was hard to say goodbye to my driver, who was in my driveway every morning and one of my closest confidants, and I worry about the girls who came to my house on Halloween expecting the lip glosses I gave away every year. I am lucky that I have a big support system and people willing to let me vent. My yoga teacher, who was highly recommended, became my life coach. It was time to adapt and adjust. It's funny how hard it is to not only be in control of your own destiny, but your own schedule as well. I was so used to every second of every day being scheduled with a meeting, photo shoot, interview, etc. I couldn't help feeling a little lost when I woke up some days and didn't have to catapult out of bed.

But you never know when some little act of kindness will change everything. A group of us went away for my husband's birthday, and one night at an outdoor dinner party the chef in charge introduced himself to me and told me his wife was a big fan of my brand. I told him of my transition and that I was thinking of doing something new. He said, 'Hey, you got this!' Every time I saw him he said it again. Soon, I started saying it back to him, 'I got this!' A few months later, I put that slogan on a sweatshirt and hat and started selling them in a concept store I was creating. Those few words gave me the confidence I needed at the time. Chef Victor was the guy I needed to see at that time.

Women are forced by societal expectations to be flexible, and constantly reinvent themselves. Having children may not change you as a person, but it certainly changes the way others look at you, and it also allows you to become, quickly, someone who is a multitasker and fast on your feet. We're also taught not to take our success for granted – which I think means you have to continue to work at it. And work harder. Just think of the adage, 'a woman's prerogative is to change her mind'! Starting over is built into our psychological DNA, and that's something we should all learn to take advantage of. Long before I left Bobbi Brown Cosmetics, I was pressing reboot on areas of my life that weren't working out for me: swapping negative relationships for newer, more positive influences; accepting when to delegate, and when to step away.

I know I have an unfair advantage when it comes to leaving one business in favour of launching another. I try to remind myself of an important approach: if everything collapses in on itself, or I realize I've made a mistake, what's the very worst thing that could go wrong? I've already achieved a lot more than I ever imagined. Recently I found myself in Whole

Foods, when I bumped into a man I'd known in a professional capacity, who was now working in the gourmet food department. I asked him what he was doing, and he explained that his company had recently gone through a round of redundancies. He didn't feel comfortable sitting at home, waiting for a new job offer to appear in his inbox, so he headed to Whole Foods and found some work to keep him occupied in the meantime. 'It's much easier to feel good about yourself if you're busy,' he said. And he's right. If things go wrong – if starting over sends you sideways – then try to keep busy. Get up and get out and you'll go forwards.

There are still moments when I can't believe how fortunate I am to be able to change my life. Change is cleansing – it's like breathing after yoga: you're getting the negative energy out, and letting the positive in. My life has gone from being very, very complicated to very, very simple and straightforward. I already feel calmer. The biggest thing I realized is that nobody is ever going to simplify my life for me. If you want a change, then you have to take the initiative, because no one else will do it for you. And if you want a fresh start, then you have to be the person who takes the risk, because otherwise, nothing will ever happen. As well as founding Bobbi Brown Cosmetics, I was beauty editor of *The Today Show* for fourteen years. When that ended, I became editor of a beauty magazine at Yahoo. And when that came to an end, I became lifestyle editor of New York's biggest radio show. Every single one of those roles was a role that I wanted – and every one was a role that I actively pitched for. The opportunities didn't come to me when I was sat at home, they came when I went after them.

TAKING A CHANCE AND STARTING OVER IS SCARY – BUT IF YOU ASK ME, HAPPINESS IS WORTH TAKING A RISK FOR.

It's easy to look at the world right now and feel like nothing's working. However, I like looking at life as an opportunity. If you aren't happy, pull back and reinvent the way you are doing things. Taking a chance and starting over is scary – but if you ask me, happiness is worth taking a risk for.

LAURA JANE WILLIAMS

LIFE LESSON NO.3
THE ART OF
LOVING YOURSELF

Babe, listen: if I've learned one thing in my life, it's that it is nobody's job to give you permission. Permission to like yourself. Permission to want what you want, and how you want it. Permission to be who you are. It's nobody's job to put you at ease, or hold your hand, or tell you – over and over again (because you never believe it the first time) – just how wonderful you are.

Does that disappoint you? Does that make you feel afraid? Fucking good. Because feeling afraid and living boldly anyway, on the terms you decide for yourself – that's how you'll learn what it is to be magic. And you, darling, are a supernatural force.

Without self-love we are neurotic and self-centred and insecure. We think we will be worthy once other people tell us we are loved. But it is you – and only you – who sets the tone for your life. To be loved we must be *loving*, and that love begins with ourselves.

If we practise self-love, everything changes. We find contentment in our work, satisfaction in our relationships, kindness for who we are and how we look and what we say. Self-love affects every aspect of our days. It isn't a privilege: it's a right.

And so, here are my sixteen tips for loving yourself, in work, friendship and romance. I haven't mastered all of them, so I certainly won't tell you to be perfect at this either. But I dip into these ideas when I can. And with self-love, every little helps. It all adds up. Self-love is cumulative.

1. Self-love doesn't always have to be 'loving' – mostly it simply has to be accepting. Self-love is an active practice, like choir rehearsal or religion: you have to keep showing up. Self-love is a verb. It is done in the 'doing'. Your work won't ever be done. You're not a project to be finished. There is no 'final level'. You can't 'win' at liking yourself – you can only keep on with keeping on, and lean into the journey of it. There is no perfect score (thank goodness).

2. Know you're worthy of your own time and energy. Anyone who was given a doll as a toddler learned, at the youngest, most impressionable age, to take care of something or someone else. Yes, it's lovely to take care of people – but we can't nourish others unless our own cup is full. When the plane crash-lands we have to fit our own oxygen mask before helping anyone else. We can't help others if we're dead. We can't champion anyone unless we're fulfilled by our own words of love and kindness and care. Self-love is the most radical act of kindness for others there is. We look after each other better once we're looking after ourselves.

3. People love you when you love yourself. And by 'love' what I really mean is respect. People respect you, and give you what you need, and appreciate you, when you do all of those things for yourself first. Your boss might need you to work late, but you must still eat a meal and take a walk for the fresh air. Your lover might be desperate to see you, but if you need a secret cinema trip for one? That's okay. Your friend might be Facetiming but just because you hear the phone ring it doesn't mean you have to answer it. Your own needs can come first.

"

YOU ARE THE
EXPERT ON YOU.
DON'T LET OTHER
PEOPLE TELL YOU
WHO YOU ARE.
DON'T LET DAVE
AT WORK MAKE
OUT LIKE YOU'RE
THE 'SENSITIVE'
ONE BECAUSE YOU
LET HIM KNOW HIS
MISOGYNIST JOKE
WAS BULLSHIT . . .

4. This links to: boundaries. Boundaries! I know! Deciding what works for you and what doesn't, and then saying it out loud. Did you know you don't have to keep your heart or mind wide open, for any dickhead in muddy boots to trample on, all in the name of being 'giving' and 'loving' and 'likeable'? Having love for yourself means learning to tell folks: 'Hey, that doesn't work for me.' You don't even have to justify why. Not feeling good for you is reason enough to say where your line is. End of. 'I can't travel 45 minutes on the Central Line to meet you for a drink, that's too far.' 'I don't want to go to Bangalore for a holiday.' 'My foundation cost £45, so no: you can't borrow it.' It's hard to set the rules, but others will know how to love you if you teach them how you love yourself. That's because . . .

5. You are the expert on you. Don't let other people tell you who you are. Don't let Dave at work make out like you're the 'sensitive' one because you let him know his misogynist joke was bullshit, or your father continue the faulty narrative that you're the 'selfish' one of his kids because you work seventy-five hours a week and so don't visit weekly like your sister. You're not 'socially awkward' because your boss said so after that work party, or 'not very sexual' because your ex-boyfriend was mad he couldn't make you orgasm with three minutes of finger-banging. YOU get to say who you are. YOU get to decide that you're empowered or daring or funny or brave or witty or sexual. Nobody knows you better than you know yourself. Trust that. Trust yourself. It's the most radical act of self-love there is to be exactly who you are, proudly.

6. Figure out who you are by figuring out who you are not. You can't be born again until you die. Admit when it sucks. Give up. Change your mind. Try something else. It will free you when you decide to no longer be tied to an idea of yourself, but rather who you really are.

7. Education, education, education. Nobody ever taught me how I'd earn and save money to afford a deposit on my own house. I wasn't taught about bringing sex toys into the bedroom to ensure I get an orgasm, either. Nobody taught me how to live in a house-share, or negotiate for a raise, or if nipple hair is normal. I've had to figure it out for myself, because I'll be damned if I'll let anybody take advantage of me because of my own ignorance. If self-respect starts anywhere, it's there: asking questions, and getting the answers. Don't rely on anybody else to teach you. Seek out knowledge yourself.

8. Be detached. You are not who you hang out with or who you date, and most of all: you are not what you do. You're so much more than all of that. They are parts of the whole, not the defining factor. Self-love is about who you are when nobody is looking. Do you remember birthdays and only say things you mean and act mindfully? Do you let yourself believe that you're allowed to want what you want? Can you find joy? Put your value in that – not in what your business card says.

9. Have goals that matter to you. If your goals aren't synched with your heart, they won't mean anything. And, if you have every excuse under the sun for why you can't fulfil your heart's desire, then baby: you just don't want it bad enough. And that's okay! You don't need to have a big old dream! Because . . .

10.   . . . You don't have to change the world to be in charge
      of yours. Some people are karmayogis – they figure
      out more about themselves through work, and so work
      becomes their driving force. It's kind of fashionable to be
      a karmayogi – or #girlboss, if you prefer. But: that doesn't
      have to be you. You don't have to be a go-getting career
      gal with high heels and even higher aspirations to be
      important. You're allowed to simply collect a paycheck,
      and then go home to knit, or cook, or train for a race, or
      get really good at gardening. You can be a beta, and still
      be in charge of your life; you can lean back and still be
      the boss of you.

11.   Don't make life more difficult than it is. The biggest lie
      we tell each other is that if it's a struggle, it's probably
      worth it. That hard work means a better payoff. That if
      it's 'too easy', it can't be real. That's bullshit. What if we
      believed life wanted us to be happy? Because she does.
      Life wants us to have all that our heart has dreamed
      of, and more. If you're pushing for something and it
      isn't making you content, ask yourself: 'Am I doing this
      because I must, or because I want to?'

12.   Say no. Say no so that your yes means something.

13.   The hardest lessons to learn are the ones your soul
      needs most. Yes, life is easy and wants you to be happy,
      but they call 'em growing pains for a reason, and that
      reason is that self-discovery can hurt. Poking around
      inside ourselves is dirty, brave work, and that's why not
      everybody does it. If something inside stings when you
      shine a light on it, it might be a sign that there's room for
      development there. You're a warrior for pushing forward
      to see how you might remedy that stinging. Good for you,
      daring woman. Good for you for not being so afraid of
      yourself that you'd rather not try at all.

YOU'RE NOT PERFECT. BUT THEN AGAIN, THE INTERESTING ONES NEVER ARE.

14. Rest is good. You know how there's corpse pose at the end of yoga, so that all the work we've done can integrate itself with the rest of our spiritual and physical selves? Sometimes we just need to *savasana* with a weekend in bed or a retreat or a walk or an afternoon with a book or five minutes with a cup of tea. Stopping still doesn't mean we're not making progress. Stopping still means progress can catch up with us.

15. Forgive yourself. You're not perfect. But then again, the interesting ones never are.

16. Self-help author Gretchen Rubin says self-love is represented in the act of striving to make ourselves happier every day. So: what do you want, in this exact moment, in order to lean in to happiness and wholeness and contentedness just a little bit more? Start there, with a baby step. Take baby steps every day, and soon you'll scale mountains. Just begin. Love yourself, and feel that love grow. There's no doubt it will. I promise.

NIMKO ALI

LIFE LESSON NO.4
**BE HONEST – EVEN
WHEN IT HURTS**

I've spoken about my fanny and my experience of female genital mutilation (FGM) a lot over the last few years. FGM is the total or partial removal of the external female genitalia for non-medical reasons. It's a really messed up form of gender-based violence, and a really, really horrid thing to happen to a child. And while these days I'm very open about my experiences and what happened to me, it hasn't always been like that.

For over twenty years I stayed silent. I told the world I was OK, while deep down I was dying. I was broken; a shell of what I projected. I lied to myself and all those around me. But while the thing that happened to me as a child was massive in scale (I mean, there are 200 million women and girls that live with FGM) the lie I was telling might seem petty. After all, it's one we all tell daily. It is one that I'm willing to bet you've said several times today. It's the lie that, 'I am OK.'

I can remember the first time I felt the impact of saying 'I am OK' when in fact I was anything but. I was eleven years old, and had been rushed into hospital with kidney failure. Four years earlier, I'd been subjected to one of the most severe forms of FGM, which had led to an infection that trickled into my blood and put my kidneys – and life – at risk. I don't remember the FGM, nor the kidney failure, feeling painful. Instead, it was the pervasive silence and total dismissal of my emotions that made me ache inside. Playing 'fine' was what hurt.

Waking up from my surgery, I felt so alone. All I wanted was a hug; for someone to tell me it was going to be OK. But everyone was freaked out. I mean, my vagina was stitched up and I am sure that would freak anyone out – I kind of understand now that it must have been a scary thing for anyone to see. But I was just eleven, and I didn't get it, and it hurt me. Looking up at the ceiling with tears rolling down my face, I was met with a stupid fake smile of reassurance; one that in turn became part of my own life for years. When I left the hospital, I left a massive part of me behind: I left the ability to express myself and react honestly. Where I once had real words and impromptu, sudden smiles I suddenly built walls.

I'd been a child – just seven – when I'd had FGM. When I returned to school after it happened and told a teacher about it and about how scared I was, she dismissed me. At the time, I thought it was because I'd explained it badly. But after leaving that hospital at the age of eleven, where doctors and nurses had seen the results of the FGM – what it was, and what it had done to me – still nobody seemed to give a fuck. I felt so alone.

So a flippant 'I'm fine' became my default response. I was full of so many questions, but I had no one to ask and no way to vocalize them. For a while, I found other, non-verbal, means of coping. The emptiness I felt could be temporarily filled with food. But that soon became an enemy too. I mean, the thing about eating non-stop to fill a bottomless emotional hole and suffocate your soul is that you put on weight. A lot of weight. You find that eating all the carbs and cakes in the house leads to your getting so fat that at thirteen years old, you can no longer celebrate Eid because nothing fits. But you still tell the world you are OK. At fourteen, I found bulimia – and for seventeen years I binged and purged, binged and purged, binged and purged. And still I told the world I was OK.

I wasn't lying to myself or those around me because I wanted to, but because I was scared. If I admitted to others (and myself) that things weren't OK, then I would have to deal with what had happened. But if the adults around me couldn't handle my FGM, then how was I supposed to?

Then the older I got, the more I read about FGM, and the more scared I became of being defined by it. Everything I read said that what had happened wasn't supposed to affect girls like me. I was cool, educated and the school netball captain. FGM was meant to happen to the girls who lived far away from England. Girls who weren't part of my daily life. My fears of being 'found out' grew and grew. It consumed me and made me doubt everything that I was, and everything that made me beautiful. I can talk about those feelings now, because I saw the same fear in someone else. Ayaan (not her real name) was a young girl I was mentoring, and she'd had the same type of FGM as me. One day, she was on stage, trying – seeking – to give a speech, explain her experience and how it affected her. As she stood on the stage shaking with people watching, I felt her fear and loneliness. In a room full of people, I found myself standing up and walking over to her as she fell apart in front of everyone. With the mic switched on, self-consciousness suddenly sidelined, I told her that she was beautiful. I told her that she was whole. As I spoke, I realized I was facing up to my own fears, too. I was being honest with myself for the first time. I'd been campaigning for FGM rights for a while by this point, but I wasn't open about my own experiences of it. I was too busy trying to appear OK, to actually work on feeling it.

Taking Ayaan aside at the end of her speech, I talked about my FGM honestly for the first time in twenty years. I told her that she was not alone and that what happened to her was awful, but did not define her. There was no personal freedom in saying those words, but I saw how it set her free to know she wasn't alone. Before that day, I'd believed that if anyone found out that I'd suffered FGM that would be it: the rest of me would be dismissed. I would be seen as nothing but a victim. I am all about my fanny now, but back then I was not ready. It took seeing Ayaan reveal her weakness, for me to admit my own.

The thing that no one tells you about life – the thing that I want to share with you now – is that no one is perfect, no one has all their shit together, and no one ever will. It's not the way humans work. Through a culmination of nature, nurture and life experiences, we're all flawed in some way. Sometimes it's your fault. Sometimes it's not. But accepting that is what makes us amazing and gives us power. I only found that power in my thirties. But it's never too late. There is so much strength in vulnerability. Letting yourself go and admitting out loud that you're not OK is always a step towards happiness. Saying you have failed doesn't make you a failure. Accepting you made a mistake is not the end of the world. Admitting that maybe, inexplicably, you just feel like shit, might make you stop feeling that way. Giving yourself a break means you can actually feel and taste life.

When you put up walls and lie to yourself and others around you, life is exhausting. You avoid forming deep or meaningful relationships because it could mean someone finding out who you are behind your boundaries. You worry beyond words for those you do love and hope they believe you when you say you are OK, lest they start to worry too. But you're crying at night, and feeling alone.

WHAT IS BRAVE IS ACCEPTING YOU'RE HAVING A HARD TIME, BUT SPEAKING UP ANYWAY. WHAT IS BRAVE IS SAYING 'I'M NOT OK.'

When I first started campaigning, I would hear the words 'brave' and 'courageous' all the time. But I was none of those things. I was coping and coasting. I was living a lie of a life, and it was not brave. I was scared. What is brave is being honest. What is brave is being you. What is brave is accepting you're having a hard time, but speaking up anyway. What is brave is saying 'I'm not OK.'

TANYA GOLD

LIFE LESSON NO.5
WHY ALCOHOL IS NO REPLACEMENT FOR LOVE

It's frightening, going insane at nineteen, but it happened to me. That was the year when I had my first alcoholic blackout. I was in my first week at university and I was drinking in the college bar. I drank easily and joyfully and without stopping. Later, I banged on the door of the room of a boy I wanted, and screamed so long and loud that the college authorities had to remove me. I only know this because I was told about it; I don't remember it. I could never tell you what happened in an alcoholic blackout; I could only imagine it, and what I imagined was terrible.

This was the beginning of the fall into insanity: if it sounds like a fairy tale, it wasn't; it was sadder and more prosaic than that. A sane woman, after that experience, would not drink alcohol again. But for me it was a trigger, a sense of coming home. For four years at university – it would have been three, but I was suspended for a year for running through the college grounds, screaming – I was almost always drunk. Afterwards, in my first few jobs in journalism, I was almost always drunk. If someone asked me why I was almost always drunk, I had no answer. I did not know why I drank. I was loved by my family; I had opportunities; there were things I could do. I can only say that it felt, to me, like fate calling. I didn't listen to anyone when they told me not to drink, because I couldn't hear them. My identity – the shiny, brave twelve-year-old girl within me – was dissolving, to be replaced with something monstrous, and she was powerful. Soon, I couldn't imagine myself any other way.

When I was sober, I was terrified because, after a while, I knew there was an assassin in my head, and it was me. With every drink she became stronger. It didn't matter if I was pretty, or smart, or met a nice boy, or got a good job. (When I was sober, I could fake sanity, and even charm.) I would inevitably lose it all, or rather throw it away, and I knew it. I built and destroyed and built and destroyed.

Quite soon, all hopes I had for myself had gone; whatever the twelve-year-old-girl had wanted, or yearned for, her world was now small and closing in. I locked myself in my mother's house, and shut the curtains, and drank beer – vodka brought me to blackout within minutes, so I turned to beer – and wondered how soon I would die of whatever was wrong with me, and whether anyone would care. I could not look at children – their innocence wounded me, for I had lost all mine – or couples: how did they manage to love each other? What did they have that I didn't? I was only twenty-seven, why was I dying, what had I done? Why was I being punished? Meanwhile, my mother dreamed of my body in a coffin.

Eventually I became too frightened to drink. Death or serious injury seemed close, and I wasn't sure I wanted it; in retrospect, I know I didn't. The twelve-year-old-girl – my best self, for she is both principled and unafraid – was stronger than I thought and the sicker I became, the more she fought to live.

I decided to spend one year without alcohol; that was all, at that time, that I could promise myself. I went to rehab in a fraying old house in Dorset and had terrible dreams – my loving sister became myself, a screaming drunk, for instance – and I ripped my scarves to pieces with my own hands. I found it comforting. As I tore the clothes I mourned myself and the people I had hurt; my amends would come later. I made no friends in rehab – I was not capable of thinking of anyone but myself – but I knew, then, that I could live without alcohol, even if happiness seemed impossible. Pride would keep me sober. Pride, and fear of madness. I read big, consuming novels and I decided to become a writer. I would remake myself – and conceal myself – with words.

Change was slow. I had taken poison for many years, and it took me twice as many years to heal, even if I could stand up, and work and smile. I learnt that you cannot remake yourself with words; you need love too. I was initially untrusting – the monster could not be a friend – and I did not get better until I learned to accept love and to believe I was deserving of it. This sounds easy on the page, but in life it was hard to do. The belief that one is unworthy of love is the central lie of the alcoholic mind. That was the drunken scream of rage outside the room of the boy at university – I don't have love. The truth is, that for at least ten years after my last drink, I was always afraid, and I was always lonely. I bore it by spending a thousand nights at the cinema, and eating. I ate the way I had drunk.

Eventually I sought out other female alcoholics and I allowed myself to love them. I do love them, for they are clever and haunted and kind, and in loving them I manage to forgive myself. They are my mirror: my dark sisters.

I never thought, when I was in the dregs of alcoholism, that I would be happy, and for many years afterwards I wasn't. Now I know that mental illness – some, not all – is something you can recover from, and even learn from. I have learnt the value of kindness. I stopped drinking still a child and now I am, at least sometimes, a woman. And I am not always afraid.

CLARA AMFO

LIFE LESSON NO.6
BE YOUR OWN BEST FRIEND

I'm my own best friend. Weirdly, it's not even a little bit scary to say that out loud any more – it's empowering. I can eat on my own, travel alone, laugh on my own and even dance on my own. Don't get me wrong, I cherish my friendships and family dearly, but one of my favourite memories from the last few years was taking myself to see the new X-Men movie for my birthday. Just me and a triple scoop of Häagen-Dazs. That simple outing felt like I'd cracked an important part of adulthood, being blissfully content with a solo visit to the movies. Happy birthday to me.

Of course I haven't always seen it this way. It's been a long road to discover the power of one. Growing up, having a best friend was a sort of status symbol, and when things went wrong, I took it as a personal attack. I used to butt heads with one of the more popular girls in my year, a typical Regina George complete with Karen and Gretchen at her side. When I was targeted, I'd always stand up for myself but some of my friends wouldn't necessarily be behind me. It was the seed of a lesson – no one *has* to do anything for you. As a teenage girl, everything feels very personal and we're socialized to fit in – nobody wants to be the outcast. But you can't expect others to fight your battles, and that's a powerful thing to discover. As the years went by, I learnt that everyone has different belief systems; just because you might lend someone a tenner for the last taxi home, the person on the receiving end might not do the same back.

But the real catalyst for change came in 2014, thanks to a guy I was seeing. I asked him why he wouldn't stay at mine overnight and he told me it was because 'it makes you like me more'. That was my lightbulb moment; if any of my friends had told me about a dude treating them that way I would have gone nuts. And I was just letting it happen. So I said 'enough', and with the help of a therapist, started to explore how I found myself on the end of that behaviour in the first place. Up until then, I would have told you that I wanted to be my own friend – but I wasn't truly treating myself as one. In fact, looking back, I'm horrified by how hard I was on myself. I had sky-high personal standards and was so afraid of letting people down that I would fester in toxic situations or waste my energy on things that upset me. For me, like many women, a large part of discovering the power of one was discovering the power to say 'no'.

Now, if something's not working for my wellbeing, I'll remove myself from that narrative. I pay close attention to what I actually want, and I don't attach stigma to a 'no'. It's not about disrespecting or disregarding someone's feelings, it's just prizing yourself. After all, I would never try to persuade a friend to do something she really didn't want to do. And it makes saying 'yes' to the things you're truly excited about that much sweeter.

But it's not about cutting yourself off from everyone else – being your own best friend means a lot of solo fun. As you get older, even arranging a bloody coffee with your mates is hard enough – if you wait for everyone's schedules to align, you're going to miss out on a lot. Now I simply ask myself 'Clara – do you want to do this?' and if the answer is 'yes', then I'm off to the cinema or club on my own, no more questions asked. I even go on holiday by myself; I've been to Jamaica and Indonesia alone, which was incredibly liberating.

YOU CAN'T EXPECT OTHERS TO FIGHT YOUR BATTLES, AND THAT'S A POWERFUL THING TO DISCOVER.

And from a practical aspect, not having to dance to anyone else's tune felt amazing – there's no getting up at 7 a.m. so you can pack in everything on the group itinerary.

Being my own best friend has also given me the courage to walk away from friendships that have run their course. Realizing some friendships are for ever but others aren't meant to last a lifetime was a true watershed moment. When I was at school, one of my best friends recounted advice from her older sister about having 'friends for a reason and friends for a season'. That line always stuck with me but I didn't fully embrace it until recently; I spent huge chunks of my life racked with guilt over friendships that were clearly dead and didn't need resuscitating. College was a turning point; friends started experimenting with things, which is completely natural but after a while I realized it wasn't for me at all. At a party one night the thought hit me: 'What am I doing here? This isn't my vibe.' So I took those feelings and had to peace out of those friendships for a while. It was hard, but people change and grow apart and that is absolutely OK. I don't mourn those endings any more. And it's far easier to stomach when you can provide your own laughter, companionship and cheerleading instead.

THERE'S ONLY ONE ME, SO I'VE LEARNT TO RATE HER. AND YOU KNOW WHAT? SHE'S ACTUALLY A PRETTY COOL PERSON.

Of course I'm not saying you don't need mates. Female friendships are so special. Thelma and Louise drove over a fucking cliff for each other – there's such a magic and subtlety in how women understand each other that I couldn't imagine not having them. In 2015 I found out my dad had died a day before I was supposed to run the Paris half-marathon with my friends. As soon as I got the dreaded phone call, my friends took over: packing my bags and buying me a ticket back to the UK. My friend Josey wouldn't let me go alone, and took the train all the way back to London with me. The circumstances weren't ideal, but that display of unwavering, unconditional friendship was one of the most beautiful moments of my life. And I'd argue that rather than competing with them, becoming your own best friend only makes these relationships stronger. If there is one thing I know for sure, it's that I can't be the best for them if I'm not OK in myself, first.

In 2016 I went back and ran the Paris half-marathon with my girls, and in 2017 I ran the Hackney half-marathon alone, and felt just as amazing as I crossed the line. I'm proud that I've learned to enjoy my own company above that of anyone else. Because no matter how much your friends love and rate you, it's pretty much useless if you can't see that in yourself. At the end of the day you come into and go out of this world alone. I used to think that was such a negative phrase. Does it mean you're not supposed to speak to people or enjoy the brilliance of your fellow humans? But now I get it. It's about understanding yourself. Accepting yourself. Valuing yourself. I celebrate the people in my life but when it comes down to it, you are your own biggest asset and the sooner you clock that, the better. All the clichés are true – life is short and life is long but there's only one me, so I've learnt to rate her. And you know what? She's actually a pretty cool person.

LUCY MANGAN

LIFE LESSON NO.7
HOW TO LIVE WITH SOMEONE WITHOUT KILLING THEM

'The way he uses the handbrake.'
'Dripping all over the bathroom after a shower.'
'His breathing.'
'Leaving one piece of washing up.'
'Her chewing.'
'The constant channel-hopping.'

These are just a few of the (printable) replies I received when I asked my girlfriends on a night out, after a bottle or six of Vino Veritas, what annoyed them about their husbands/wives/long-term partners. 'Breathing' actually made several appearances. Breathing seems to be a big one. 'In the evenings,' one specified. 'The evenings are the only time.'

She said this with an air of generosity, and this is why my friends are my friends. They understand, without anything needing to be said, that there just are times in life when to be with someone is to consider the fact that you only find yourself becoming murderous over their continued respiration in the evening a mark of both benevolence and success.

Because the truth of the matter is – life is hard, and life with someone else in it is even harder. The ideal, we are told and sold on over the years, is that (after a few false starts and kerrazy *Sex and the City/New Girl*-type adventures – delete according to generation) you find your soulmate and settle down to enjoy the bliss of perfect communion with another person for the rest of your long, gilded, smiling-adoringly-at-each-other-over-breakfast lives together.

And like most ideals, it is a load of cockamamie bullshit that does nothing more than set you up for failure.

It took me many years to realize that the myth of perfect happiness in a relationship was just that – a myth. I thought it was all down to my naturally unsociable, mistrustful and emotionally cauterized temperament, which means that I generally feel the presence of other people as little more than a parade of intrusions upon my privacy, depredations on my solitude, shatterings of my peace and tolls on my personal equilibrium and autonomy. And for sure, this is part of it.

But, first of all, this is true for a lot of people, so it needs to be openly acknowledged as a genuine and legitimate difficulty. And I think it needs open acknowledgement particularly for and among women, most of whom (and I include myself in this) are powerfully socialized to 'make nice', be tolerant, give of themselves and grease the wheels of other people's lives in a way that men, generally speaking, are not. And when that labour (and any behaviour that arises from external messages rather than your own inclinations IS labour, though it may be so constant that it barely registers as such any more) starts being necessary at home as well as in public and at work – well, my dears, I think we can forgive ourselves for starting to chafe.

Second of all – we know that human beings are not designed to live in perfect harmony. Look at the world around you. Look at your family. Look at your friends. Can you point to anyone you have known longer than ten minutes, anyone you care about and say that you've never had a row with them? Why are we suddenly supposed to make an exception for one person? Especially one who insists on laying his trousers along the wardrobe shelf instead of hanging them up like any normal person? Or who puts leftover sausage back in the fridge not in Tupperware or even on a plate but directly onto the wire shelf? Or who for the last five years has wanted to move said fridge next to the kettle so that it blocks the only window in the room but means his milk will get into his tea five nanoseconds faster?

I'm sorry – where was I?

Ah yes; not being designed to live in perfect harmony with another. Over the years, it has become clear that there is nothing wrong with my heart, my mind, my soul – or my marriage. It is simply absolutely, completely and utterly normal to find living with someone periodically enraging. Sometimes for short periods. Sometimes for long periods. Sometimes for long periods that join up and feel like they are never going to end. A friend of mine once, during one of the latter, used to daydream about her partner 'just stepping off a kerb and being run over by a lorry. Sometimes he dies, sometimes it just puts him in hospital for a year and I have the house to myself. Depends what kind of day I'm having.' Another used to comfort herself with the thought that hers 'might just be one of those men that disappear one day and you never see them again. I mean, somehow I'll know he's safe, just gone off to start another life without telling me. It's all good.'

It is stories like these that make the myth crumble and enable you to carry out the necessary emotional recalibration to carry on with life as it is lived in reality.

To be clear – I am not talking about the stress, frustration, rage, misery and despair that is caused by being with the wrong person (and/or denying to yourself that you are with the wrong person). That is an entirely different matter, and the terribly complicated, terribly simple answer there is to be brave and listen to what your heart is telling you as soon as you can bear to, because it will always find a way to be heard, and the longer you avoid it the more catastrophic the consequences will be.

I am talking only about the ways in which relationships diverge from the image of perfection we are brought up with. Freeing yourself from the expectation of perfection in any area is, I think, the greatest gift a woman can give herself, especially in this day and age when galleries of carefully curated images are warping our views of what is achievable in ever more fields of endeavour. I wish I had realized decades earlier that the world would not end if I was not the perfect student, the perfect daughter (actually, then it might have – my mother is VERY tough), the perfect shape, the perfect law trainee, the perfect host, the perfect writer. I lost an incomputable amount of time and energy chasing impossible ideals instead of realizing that 'good enough' is – well, good enough, and in fact aiming for that usually allows you to perform better than aiming for perfection and constantly being consumed by guilt and anxiety when you fail at every turn.

There is one complicating factor I do think worth mentioning. Utterly natural, unavoidable emotional troughs in a relationship exist but can always be aggravated by external factors, like job stress, illness in the family and so on. But most commonly for women living with men specifically, in my direct and anecdotal experience, it is the fact that their pot of goodwill tends already to be more depleted than their partners' because they are already doing a lot more of the unsung work therein. We still do more than half the housework (we will know feminism has completed its work when there is not a man left in the world who doesn't clean his own shit off the toilet after – well, AFTER) and – an educated guess – about 80 per cent of the emotional labour required to keep a couple and a household together. The keeping track of birthdays, sorting out presents, arranging vet appointments for pets, booking holidays, researching the vaccinations needed, managing social invitations and attendant reciprocal gestures – these fall disproportionately to women and, contrary to opinion apparently prevalent in the world of the penis-sporter, are not immensely enjoyable or fulfilling in themselves. If you are doing too much of that for too long, it can make you a tad quicker to anger than you might otherwise be.

But after you have recognized this (and reorganized your – and his – life accordingly), you can still be sustained by the knowledge that the perfect relationship does not exist. We are imperfect beings in an imperfect world. Happiness comes from a fair distribution of labour, to be sure, but also by not cleaving to a fiction and not getting spooked by reality. Explicable (caused by excessive *Seinfeld* watching, absurd sausage placement, fridge relocation and trouser-storage stupidity) and inexplicable (breathing in the evenings – it IS annoying, but they've got to do it) spousal rage is okay. Don't be afraid. Hold hard. It doesn't mean anything beyond the fact that you are – both – human. You will be back to whatever your normal is in time.

Try not to say or do anything that will have repercussions lasting longer than the spasm of fury itself. You can say, for example, through gritted teeth, 'I am not having the discussion about the fucking fridge/sausages/trousers again', but not, 'It is exactly this kind of total cretinism that makes me wish I had never met you, never got myself trapped in this abyss walled by futile explanation and negotiation out of which I fear I will never climb. I honestly wouldn't piss on you if you were on fire right now.' For example. For example.

Keep calm. And carry on. This too, my darlings, will pass. Any day now, I'm hoping. Any day now.

JO CLIFFORD

LIFE LESSON NO.8
YOU CAN'T CHOOSE WHO YOU ARE

Something that often gets said to us trans people is that 'you can't choose your own gender'.

And they're right. You can't choose.

I know this because I tried. I tried to choose. I spent nearly fifty years of my life trying to be a man, when I wasn't. So I know our gender identity is something far deeper than our conscious intent.

It all started very young. I must have been about four when I looked in the mirror and didn't really recognize the boy I saw there. I can look back on that now and say this was the first sign of what we now call gender dysphoria but at that time, in the early fifties, such terms weren't around. Words like 'transgender' and 'transsexual' didn't exist either, so neither I nor my parents had any means of comprehending this. All I could do was hope it would go away and try to be 'normal'.

But it didn't go away. And when I was a teenager and playing girls' parts in the school plays I knew, somehow, I'd be happier living as a girl.

I was so horrified and guilty and ashamed that I did everything I could to suppress it. I tried as hard as I could to grow up to be a normal man.

I failed, of course. There was something non-negotiable about this. It was certainly far, far stronger than I was.

But although the next forty long years brought me much suffering, they brought much joy as well. And looking back, it's clear to me that it's only through living through all those years that I could find the courage and the strength to become the person I am today. A woman feeling happy in her own skin . . .

The first thing was that I fell in love. It was love at first sight for me when I first saw Susie, and love at first sight for her as well.

One of the horrible things about transphobia is that it gets inside you and makes you think yourself a horrible person. Someone who could certainly never be loved. And yet Susie loved me.

I hadn't told anybody about myself before I met her, and I'd thought that if anyone knew I'd die of shame. But I knew I had to tell her; and when I did, soon after we got into bed together, she said: 'I've always known there was something very feminine about you, and that's one reason why I love you.'

And when she said that, she saved my life.

We were together for thirty-three years, until she died of a brain tumour, and in that time I think I must have helped her discover herself to be the feminist historian she eventually became. I know she certainly helped me become a writer.

Best of all, we had two daughters together. Being a feminist, she absolutely was not willing to abandon her career as a journalist and devote herself to childcare. I didn't want to devote my life to being a breadwinner either; so we literally divided the working week in two, and for one half I looked after the children while she worked, and for the other half she looked after the children while I worked. We were both struggling freelance writers; and we both became struggling freelance parents. And it worked.

I so loved looking after my daughters. I was brought up to believe childcare was women's work; and so being so thoroughly engaged in it was a very powerful way of expressing the woman inside me. And it was good for all of us.

Somehow through all that I became a playwright, and a successful one, too. When I write plays, I always become the characters in my imagination, and the actors performing them too. Whenever I could I gave a woman the central role; and made sure there were as many women as men in the cast. And I would go off writing in a private room, where I always wore a skirt or a dress.

So although I was still in the closet, I was still able to express the woman inside me.

By my early fifties I seemed to have it all: a happy marriage, two beautiful daughters, and a successful writing career. But somehow it all felt very wrong. I wasn't being true to myself; and I started to have breakdowns.

I was a university professor when the worst one happened. I'd turned up for work at the start of a new term, and couldn't understand the timetable. And then I started crying and couldn't stop.

A wise friend told me to go home and rest, and I did that. That night I had a dream: I was driving along a motorway, on a bridge going over a steep valley high in the mountains. Only the road had suddenly stopped. When I got out of the car and went to take a look, I found myself looking down into an abyss.

Then I looked around me and saw that the other carriageway kept going. That I would have to struggle over some rubble and some very rough ground, but that I could join it. And then my journey could go on. When I thought about it all the next morning, I understood it to mean that my life as a man had come to an end. That what I needed to do, finally, was to make the change. That I needed to start living as a woman.

And then my life could go on.

This conformed to a growing sense that I think we'd both had growing in us over the past few years; but had both been afraid of and had been trying to hard to deny.

When I told Susie she was deeply distressed by it. She said that if I became a woman she couldn't see how we could go on being together. That she loved me and needed me as a man.

I was so distressed, too. At the same time all the transwomen I had met back then seemed sadly embittered and unhappy people. After spending half of my life trying hide my female identity, I didn't want to spend the second half of my life trying to hide the fact I had once been male.

And our love for each other was so profoundly important to us. So I put off the change yet again; and I am so glad I did, because it wasn't that long afterwards that she was diagnosed with the brain tumour that was to kill her. And we could face it together, and I could look after her till the end.

One night quite soon after her diagnosis I remember being horribly unhappy. It was horrible that she was going to die. And her illness meant we could no longer sleep together, and I so badly missed her.

I heard a voice that night. A voice speaking quite distinctly inside my head. And the voice said: 'The woman inside you is wholly good. She will help you through the pain of the next few months; and she will help you build a new life once Susie has gone.'

And that's how it's turned out. After Susie's death, when I told my daughters I could no longer go on living as a man, I said I didn't know what would happen or quite what would become of me, but one thing was for sure, I would always love them, and I would always be their dad.

Which I am. And they call me dad and refer to me as she, often in the very same sentence, and when they say it, it makes absolute sense.

Which, of course, it does.

Susie was terrified that if I lived as a woman I would ruin my life, and I feared the same thing too. 'John Clifford' was very successful in his way, and though he was unhappy in many ways, he could deal with that unhappiness, sort of. Whereas Jo . . . Jo was a complete step into the unknown. Who knew where she would end up?

Turns out, she found a good place. It amazes me how happy I am in my skin. And because I like myself so much more, it seems to be easier for people to like me. And that means I truly value my work; and that makes it easier for other people to value my work too.

It's very hard to become one's own self. The world told me so fiercely and persistently I was a boy, and my body said the same. I had to struggle very hard to listen and respect the inner voice that so quietly and so persistently told me I wasn't a boy at all.

I felt so alone. But what I've come to understand is that we all have to do it.

We all have to learn, somehow, to disentangle the false from the true and become our own real selves. Because this isn't just about being trans. This is also about being human.

**JESS
PHILLIPS**

LIFE LESSON NO.9
**SAY SOD IT
AND TAKE A RISK**

66

'Sod it. What's the worst that could happen?'

This small (but potentially fatal) phrase is the beginning, middle and end of why I have ever had any kind of success in my life. I am a natural risk-taker. I'm addicted to jeopardy. And while what I am writing right now may come back to bite me on the bum and be a cautionary tale for the future, I'll take my chances. The bravura girl who had it all and lost it all. Time will tell I suppose. For now I'll rest easy on my ample laurels and make the case for bravado.

Generally speaking, the common view seems to be that women take fewer risks in life than men. Like all of those who follow their hearts quicker than following their heads, I have undertaken no such longitudinal study to find out if that's true or not. Instead, I just Googled 'Do women take fewer risks?'

The first page of results are, you probably won't be shocked to hear, entirely useless. Something from the *Telegraph* saying that women are more risk averse. Something from the *Daily Mail* saying 'one expert disagrees'. Now, I've mentioned that I like a risk, but even I am not slapdash enough to take these as sources to live by. If I did I would have spent the last ten years changing my red wine-drinking habits weekly; one day it kills us, the next week it's *aqua de vie*.

But I did find one seemingly good source, from a man called Doug Sundheim, who actually conducted a study which was published in the *Harvard Review*. He suggests that women and men take just as many risks as one another. It's just that the risks are *different* risks. And like everything that women do, like women's work and women's health, the risks taken by women are barely considered risks at all. In fact, they're considered a normal part of life for women and girls.

Historically, whenever a woman does anything, it's ignored, degraded or seen as intrinsically less worthwhile than when a man does something. Y'know, because of sexism and all that jazz. Women are not too weak, too mild or too delicate to succeed. We're just unfortunate enough to live in a society that still sees masculine activity, strategy and attitude as the only attributes worth celebrating. And in a world where a person's worth is defined by money and power, risks undertaken by sharp-suited, quick-witted city slickers betting away the nations finances become the good kind of risk. The right kind of risk. The kind of risk that could cost you something.

Admittedly, some of the work I have done in Parliament around women in the workplace leads me to think that women are less likely to take risks in their careers than men. Recently, while on the Women and Work All Party Parliamentary Group, a woman from a bank informed me that when considering business start-up loans, women often have to be encouraged to borrow more – to be bolder, to take bigger risks. Yet all my years working at Women's Aid told me a completely different story. It taught me that when it comes to their relationships and personal lives, women will risk almost anything – both for themselves, and for their families. And I know from both my own experience and many years of working with them, that young women live their lives walking a tightrope of independence in the face of risk. Even going on a night out presents us with a great many. Nevertheless, we are not all locked away, cross-stitching tapestries like nuns in a bid to avoid them. So women can take risks thank you very much. If anything, we ace it.

Now that we've established that we can get back to where we began: saying 'sod it'. It may well be because I bore easily that I run towards new opportunities. It may be because I am a show off, a peacock (not a hen) who feasts on entertaining anecdotes and the ability to say 'I did that' to my assembled friends. But whatever the reason is, I like to scare myself by agreeing to do and try new things. When I was a kid I was heralded by my family as being brave and bold. I would always climb to the highest summit, take the trickiest route in an adventure playground, join in with older kids and stand my ground in an argument. My parents would take pictures of me hanging from a high wire, beaming. They asserted their pride to me and bragged to their friends about my courage. My seemingly ridiculous ability to take a risk was rewarded with endlessly positive affirmations. Now, I'm no psychologist but if you grew up as the youngest of four siblings and the only girl, you're bound to seek out opportunities to do what the big boys do – and you learn pretty quickly that if you want to get a slice of the limelight, then you have to really shine. My childhood may have provided fertile ground to make me a risk-taker but it wasn't an attribute I was born with, just as I don't believe it comes naturally to anyone. Now, just as then, I choose to be brave because of the benefits it bestows upon me.

One of the biggest personal risks I've ever taken came at twenty-two. I was in a new relationship when I discovered I was pregnant – and conveniently it was in the same week that I was being evicted from my home. With a deep breath, I moved in with my brand-new boyfriend and decided to change my entire life overnight. Gone was the partying barmaid/office temp, and in was the unemployed mother of an infant. But when the two blue lines appeared on the urine-soaked stick I didn't for a second think it was a huge decision that would require weeks of debate. Instead, I felt thrilled. Not thrilled like posh people say when they hear good news ('Oh dahling, we are so super-duper thrilled for you'), but a sense of thrill as from an adventure that would make cracking anecdotes. Having a baby was the last thing I was expecting, or that anyone expected of me. I was a clever girl who had a successful career stretching out in front of me. Having a baby would damage my prospects, plunge me into relative poverty and put the kibosh on all of my plans. But I did it anyway.

Later in life, I did it again – potentially on an even larger scale. When I decided to stand as a candidate in the 2015 election I risked my family's income and the home we had managed to scrimp and save to buy. Both my husband and I took a pay cut in order to change our working hours, and we financed a lot of the campaign ourselves – all the while facing the possibility that absolutely none of it would pay off if I lost the race. But when people ask me how my husband and I made the decision (one that would take me away from my children to live in another city, should I win), they seem to want to hear that it was carefully thought through while sitting around the kitchen table with a spreadsheet. The reality is that I took a phone call one night from someone in the Labour Party suggesting that I might think about putting myself forward for selection. 'Obviously you will have to talk it over with your family,' he said. While still on the phone I shouted down the stairs to my husband Tom: 'I'm thinking of putting myself forward to be an MP, what do you think?' 'Yeah, sounds good,' he yelled back. That was it. No hand wringing, no 'what ifs'. Just a decision made quickly, simply because it was exciting.

So yeah, I have never been a planner. I am a coper, and a catcher, but not a planner. When life throws things at me I jump up to grab them – rather than protecting my head and flinching away. But I am brave by choice, not design, and I feel scared all the time. Often after a decision is made or a deed is done, I have to fight off endless guilt and anxiety. What if it was a decision poorly made? What if it's too late to change my mind? But I've learned to use my fear to motivate me. The very same day that I was picked as the candidate for my seat in the 2015 election, I almost instantly crashed from the excitement. I remember sitting in our local café with my husband and insisting that I had almost certainly signed our divorce papers by making this decision. No matter if there was evidence to the contrary, all I could think of were MPs who had had affairs and all the Westminster relationships that had cracked wide open under the pressure and long periods of absence. Talking about these fears was the only way to overcome them. My husband, family and mates would just roll their eyes and tell me to stop being so dramatic. And when they challenged me with the option of changing my mind, to drop out, to give up, that always seemed way more terrifying. I guess what I am trying to say is that while I take a risk willingly I love to moan on about it afterwards. I'm scared just like everyone else.

Nor am I a hapless risk-taker who needlessly puts herself in harm's way. I am a quick-thinking risk assessor, who turns fear into action in most cases. As soon as I start to feel fear, I tell myself to be brave. Sometimes it's a small act, such as daring to be the person on the train who tells the gang of young kids to turn off their annoying music, or jumping out of my car in traffic because someone is being beaten up outside a pub. Sometimes it's bigger than that. Sometimes it's a matter of saying 'yes'. Yes, I will give up everything to start a new life, live a new dream.

Of course, it would be crass to underplay the need for support when taking a risk. People believing in me and willing me forward have carried me through the most white-knuckle risks I have taken in my life. Having a safety net of people, money or security gives you a soft landing for your biggest leaps. And alas, this means that often the same people who already have so much can also risk it all in order to double up their successes. I couldn't have taken the risks I have without supportive family, friends and colleagues – along with the knowledge that when all was said and done, I would never ever be totally destitute.

But I still stand by my belief. We women are masters in the art of risk, for fear is – for many of us – a natural part of life. Whether it's fear about our personal safety, fear for our families or fear of letting people down, we're used to pushing through and carrying ourselves forwards in the face of danger. And we should use that fear to drive us forward, to help us fight back, to force us to thrive. Because being a woman is a risky business. So it's time to say, 'Sod it, I'll give it a go.'

After all, what's the worst that could happen?'

FEARLESS WOMEN WHO TOOK ON PARLIAMENT

EMILY DAVISON
(1872–1913)

Most often remembered as the Suffragette who threw herself under the King's horse in 1913, Emily Davison is one of history's leading figures in the fight for women's rights. On the evening of the 1911 census, Emily famously hid in a broom cupboard in Parliament so the next day she could list her address as 'House of Commons'. The message was a powerful one – women claim the same political rights as men.

NANCY ASTOR
(1879–1964)

The first ever female MP entered the Commons in 1919 when US aristocrat Nancy Astor took up her Conservative seat. Despite the hostility from male colleagues, Astor was a fervent advocate for the rights of women, supporting lowering the legal age of women voters from thirty to twenty-one (the act passed in 1928), the expansion of nursery education and for more women to be recruited across the civil service.

BARBARA CASTLE
(1910–2002)

Known as the 'Red Queen' thanks to her socialist beliefs and flaming red hair, Barbara Castle became the first ever female minister of state when she took on the role of Minister of Transport in 1965. In Parliament, she helped to pass the Equal Pay Act in 1970 and to introduce child benefits to all children in 1975, which, crucially, were paid to mothers rather than fathers.

MAUREEN COLQUHOUN
(born 1928)

Maureen Colquhoun became Britain's first openly lesbian MP one year after being selected in 1974. Passionate about feminism, Colquhoun fought for crèche facilities for female delegates at the 1975 Labour conference and asked the Commons speaker to refer to her as 'Ms' – the first person in Parliament ever to do so. Colquhoun was eventually deselected in 1977 by her party members for her 'obsession with trivialities such as women's rights' – yet she continued to work as a political activist until her retirement.

MARGARET THATCHER
(1925–2013)

Margaret Thatcher didn't just make waves in Britain when she became the UK's first female Prime Minister, she made them across the world. Whether you liked her policies or not, Conservative Thatcher became the twentieth century's longest-serving British PM. In the words of Cherie Blair QC: 'At a time when there were more MPs called John than women MPs, Thatcher broke the glass ceiling.'

CHRISTINA LAMB OBE

LIFE LESSON NO.10

FINDING HOPE IN TIMES OF DESPAIR

My job is to go where wars are. I fly to places where normal people are leaving.

Sometimes I look around at other people serving in shops or suited up, travelling with briefcases on the tube to their offices, and wonder about having a normal life with a job where you just go to work and come back at the end of the day. Where you don't have to worry about being shot at or suicide bombed or kidnapped or ending up in one of those videos with a knife across your throat.

Occasionally, for 'a break', I get natural disasters – earthquakes, floods, even a famine.

In my fridge, between bottles of sauvignon blanc and tomato ketchup, is a cholera vaccine. And in my wardrobe, where most women keep their little black dress, I keep a flak-jacket.

Sometimes it leads to extreme situations. On 18 October 2007, when I should have been at my son's parents', evening, I was on board Benazir Bhutto's bus when it was blown up in the biggest bomb in Pakistan's history.

I'd known Benazir for twenty years – in fact she had a huge impact on my career. In 1987 I got to interview her when I was starting out as an intern on the *Financial Times* and she was Pakistan's opposition leader, exiled in the UK. The day of our interview was the day she announced her engagement to Asif Ali Zardari, and a few months later a beautiful, gold-inscribed invitation landed on my doormat to her wedding in Karachi.

That wedding was my first introduction to Pakistan. Not only was it incredibly colourful, but every night after the ceremony there were gatherings with her political colleagues to discuss toppling Pakistan's then military dictator, General Zia.

Covering local news in Birmingham, which I was doing by then as a trainee news reporter for Central TV, suddenly seemed very boring. Moreover, as the only young female in the newsroom located in an area with many motorway crashes, I kept landing the awful job of going to the houses of victims and asking their families for photos.

So I moved to Pakistan and started work as a foreign correspondent, even though in those days I had no idea what foreign correspondents did. I started travelling across the border into Afghanistan with the mujahedin fighting the Russians. Shortly after that in August 1988, General Zia died in a mysterious air-crash – caused by a box of exploding mangoes – and Benazir became Prime Minister. But it wasn't long till the army saw her off again. Eventually she ended up back in exile in London. When in 2007 she decided to return home again after nine years away, she asked me to go with her.

I wasn't intending to be on her bus. Over that year I'd had several narrow escapes – I'd been ambushed by the Taliban in Helmand and was in a hotel in Peshawar which was suicide bombed. And when I interviewed her in London, on the eve of her return, Benazir told me she'd had lots of assassination threats. So my plan was to go on the media bus behind.

Then we landed in Karachi and I saw the crowds, with her standing on top of the bus. And I knew I had to be there.

It was fine to start with. The atmosphere was electric. Benazir was overjoyed to be back. There were huge crowds, people everywhere, on roofs, up trees, clinging onto lamp-posts; there was music playing, even doves were being released.

But I could see that on an open-top bus we were very exposed, particularly as the route to the Jinnah mausoleum where she was due to speak took us under fifteen bridges and flyovers. I asked the head of security how he would protect Benazir and he said, 'It's in God's hands' – which wasn't very reassuring.

With so many people in the street our progress was so slow that it got dark. Benazir pointed out to me that the streetlights kept going off. Also, the jammers which were supposed to block any remote signals that could set off pre-planted bombs were clearly not functioning as all our mobile phones were working.

However, there was so much excitement and the journey went on so long – nine hours in total, so that we had to order in pizzas on the bus, and were joking about needing breakfast too – that I forgot about the danger.

So it was a complete shock when suddenly there was a low boom, like a steel door scraping across concrete. The bus lurched and the music stopped.

I'd been near suicide bombings before and knew there is often a second, bigger blast so I shouted to stay down.

Then within a minute there was a second explosion, much louder, and orange flames everywhere. Then silence. Then sirens.

I was terrified that the fuel tank would catch fire. We didn't know it was in a special lead casing. So we all jumped off the top then ran like crazy, through all the blood and plastic sandals and body parts.

There were 150 people killed that night. Afterwards, washing off flecks of other people's burnt flesh in the shower, I thought, 'That's it.' I'd already had way more than my nine lives and wondered if it was time to quit.

But on my first evening back in London, I went to a dinner to honour Beatrice Mtetwa, a brave human rights lawyer from Zimbabwe, a beautiful country that descended into cash-strapped chaos following President Mugabe's relentless seizure of white-owned farms and his refusal to relinquish power. It's a country I have reported from a lot, bearing witness to the droughts, state-sponsored violence and horrific levels of starvation, even though British journalists were banned and I'd been named an enemy of the state – accused of writing about 'corpses on golf courses'.

I told her I couldn't see the point in going there undercover and putting people at risk in talking to me when it didn't make any difference. She told me: 'If people like you don't report, what's the point of people like me doing what we're doing?'

I thought about the Lorax from Dr Seuss's books, who said: 'Unless someone like you cares a whole awful lot, nothing is going to get better. It's not.'

But more and more I wonder, is bearing witness enough? What's the point of exposing atrocities if nothing is done about them?

Over the last few years I have seen and heard some of the most horrific things in my career. In northern Nigeria in April 2014, in the small town of Chibok, more than 200 girls were abducted by Boko Haram from their school dormitory, making headlines all over the world for a couple of weeks. I later found that thousands more had been abducted unreported. Some had since been freed in military operations and were in camps and told me of how they'd been raped, forced to marry Boko Haram fighters, and then, when they escaped, their own family wouldn't take them back, fearing they had been indoctrinated or seeing them as sullied.

Then there were the Yazidis – 5,000 women abducted by ISIS and sold into sex slavery for as little as the price of a cigarette packet. About 3,000 have now escaped or been freed. One of them, a sixteen year old, told me the worst moment of her time as a sex slave was when her captor, a fat judge, brought back a ten year old and raped her all night in the adjoining room as she cried for her mother.

But when people ask me why I do it – that's easy. Because in the darkest skies, you often find the brightest stars. When I feel overwhelmed, I look for the helpers – the people who push onwards, and whose hope can teach us all.

After the Taliban fell in 2001, turning down Blood Bank road in Herat brought me to a group of women writers who had risked their lives to study literature. Realizing the only thing women were allowed to do by the Taliban was sew, they had set up something called the Golden Needle Sewing School. It was run by a professor of literature and under their sequins and material, they smuggled books by James Joyce and Virginia Woolf. They never made a single dress.

A few years ago I was lucky enough to work with Malala Yousafzai, who risked her life to go to school. Yet despite having been shot she shows no bitterness. She even says she would like to meet the gunmen and explain why it's important for girls to go to school – if for no other reason than that their sisters and mothers can be treated by female doctors.

Then there was Nujeen, an amazing Syrian refugee who crossed from Aleppo to Cologne in a wheelchair, always with a smile on her face. She told me how she educated herself from television, because she couldn't go to school – which meant she learned English from American soap-operas; how she wondered why food in Europe doesn't look like it does on *Masterchef*; and about the way she listed the Romanov tsars to relieve stress while on the boat making the dangerous crossing to Greece.

Or the widows of Lesbos who helped refugees on the beach, giving them dry clothes and warm drinks and most important of all a hug to show they are not forgotten.

Recently in Afghanistan I met an amazing group of women cyclists who bike through the streets, despite men throwing stones at them and shouting abuse. They told me they see what they are doing as part of women's struggle and on the bikes they feel as if they are flying.

Best of all were the Guitar Girls of Kabul. Street kids who scraped a living selling chewing gum or scarves, they had all lost brothers and sisters to suicide bombs. Many were survivors of attacks themselves. Yet they had the biggest smiles on their face when they played 'Fragile' by 'Sting from England'.

Those are the stories I want to bring home in my suitcase. For they give me faith in humanity. Their resilience in the face of adversity shows we are all stronger than we think.

Is it a coincidence that they are all women? It seems to me that women are often the real heroes of war. They are the ones who protect, feed and educate their children when all hell is breaking loose around them.

Over and over again, I've seen how women working together can be a great force. I've learned how we all want the best for our children, wherever we are. And that one person or one small act can make a difference.

When you think of war you might think of guns and bombs and danger and death. I think of those things too, and I hate those things. But I also think of these people.

When you are living through a war, the small things that often preoccupy us in everyday life – a train running late or a person irritating you – don't really matter. Instead you rejoice in what one of the Guitar Girls described to me as 'finding a yellow flower among the rubble'.

Unfortunately, the longer I work as a war correspondent, the more wars there seem to be to cover, particularly in the Middle East, and they never seem to end. They spill over back home in the UK in the form of refugees, or sometimes even as attacks in restaurants or shopping malls or concerts, places that are supposed to be safe – making victims out of people who never thought to be caught up in faraway wars.

Sometimes, such as when I've walked through the old city of Aleppo, seeing street after ancient street reduced to rubble, and thinking of all the many thousands who have been killed or wounded, it can be hard to find a bright spot. Even some of those who tried to bring joy – such as the Clown of Aleppo, who dressed up for children under siege – lost their lives. Then you come across one old man who has opened a falafel shop amid the ruins, feeding the few who still live there.

In this time of 'fake news' and 'alternative facts', where different is too often seen as dangerous, these real people with real stories are what I believe we really need to hear to give us hope in the future. In the end we are all looking for that yellow flower. It's by listening to their experiences that we can find it.

5 WAYS YOU CAN MAKE A DIFFERENCE

1. Help UK women unlock their potential

Smart Works is a UK charity that provides high-quality clothes, styling advice and interview training to help women into work while boosting their self-belief and confidence. From unused workwear to good quality accessories, this is the place to put those preloved items to good use.
smartworks.org.uk

2. Give girls across the world an education

In 2012, fifteen-year-old Malala Yousafzai was shot by a gunman on her way to school in Pakistan for daring to blog about life under the Taliban. While recovering, she was sent to the UK for treatment and safety; two years later she was awarded the Nobel Peace Prize. Now, the Malala Fund she co-founded with her father works to ensure all girls complete twelve years of free, safe, quality education.
malala.org

3. Keep freedom of speech alive

Foreign correspondent Marie Colvin was killed on assignment in Homs, Syria, in 2012. The Marie Colvin Memorial Fund was set up by her family to reflect her lifelong dedication to human rights, humanitarian aid, education and journalism.
mariecolvin.org

4. Teach a family to farm

Heifer International, a global organization with programmes operating across Africa, Asia and the Americas, has a 'pass it forward' approach. With a focus on women – who produce 80% of the developing world's food – Heifer trains families to farm sustainably. They then teach their neighbours the same skills, kick-starting a thriving trade community.
heifer.org

5. Support modern slavery survivors

It's predicted that there may be as many as 13,000 victims of modern slavery in the UK alone. Unseen UK, a charity that supports survivors to lead independent lives, has created innovative ways that we can all make a difference, from buying a reusable cup, sponsoring a room in one of their refuges, or volunteering in their office.
unseenuk.org

ALIX FOX

SIX THINGS I'VE LEARNED ABOUT LOVE

I am a woman who is rarely listless.

By which I don't mean that I'm never lethargic or sluggish. No: I mean, I love making lists. I find it cathartic, constructive and calming to fire out the contents of my head in neat bullet points, whether they are tasks I want to complete, cross out and forget – or things I wish to remember.

I began my 'Waiting List' in 1996, aged fourteen. It's a record of everyone I have ever been romantically or sexually involved with, while I wait to meet the exceptional individual who will draw the list to a close. Currently, there are forty-nine names on it. I maintain that I've learned lessons from each and every one of them, whether all we shared was an ephemeral kiss, or we contemplated sharing a surname.

To prove my theory, I picked six at random, and wrote down everything they taught me, from the hilarious to the heart-wrenching. I believe it is a list worth listening to.

Number 28

It was as though he'd been concocted in a laboratory, specially grown in a petri dish to cater to my predilections. Tall as Rapunzel's tower, with entertaining stories longer than her hair. A knack for unearthing quirky knick-knacks in second-hand shops, which he'd send me along with first-rate letters. Passionate and compassionate, laidback yet lively. Lovely.

Number 28 reckoned I'd been custom-blended to please his palate, too. We were excited to get together; so convinced we had the makings of something marvellous. But then . . . meh. What we'd expected to be fantastic was strangely flaccid.

Sometimes, a relationship can look perfect on paper, but when you try to fold that paper into an aeroplane, it simply doesn't fly. However hard you try, it never quite takes off.

It's baffling – exasperating – when your heart smarts to be with someone, and you find a person who in theory seems tailor made, only to try them on for size and find that, inexplicably, they don't suit you.

The chemistry of love is infinitely more complex and unpredictable than any physical science. There is no periodic table that can neatly inform you of all the elements required for a spellbinding romance, nor how to recognize and properly combine each rapturous reagent. Periodically, I've drunk myself under the table in mourning over this.

Yet like it or not, at times love functions more like magic than logic. However much you try to reason and rationalize about the factors and circumstances that *ought* to conjure it up, like a rabbit in a hat, it will spring from where you least expect it – and be absent from where you felt sure it made sense for it to dwell. The best you can do is recognize and accept this – absurd, infuriating and disappointing as it is. Doggedly trying to force a connection rarely works. Carrying around an empty top hat seldom summons a rabbit.

Indeed, holding onto an empty hat feels painfully like begging.

Put it down.

Number 17

Ah, we never made each other laugh, 17 and I.

If you don't ever crack up with them, break up with them. When your heart is maximally, brimmingly, burstingly full, your sides will split and your ribs will ache.

GSOH or GTFO.

Number 35

The saddest vending machines in the world are in hospital waiting rooms. They weep thin streams of PG Tips into plastic cups the colour of prosthetic limbs. Deliriously exhausted, dizzily fretful people sip at these insipid beakers of lukewarm, attempted normality, staring into the middle distance, trying to breathe through the high-pitched hiss of panic that accompanies emergency.

After eighteen months with Number 35, I was the human embodiment of that tragic cup of tea: a fragile beige vessel filled with misery, pantomiming that everything was OK in the midst of a blaring breakdown.

Crying in the shower became routine. Sob, rinse, repeat. I got to know the precise acoustics of how a desperate wail echoes when confined to a tiled, wipe-clean room. I would stand beneath the stream until I was numb enough to get out and get on. I wasn't actively suicidal, but I would often think about how comfortably convenient it would be if I hadn't woken up that morning; what peaceful relief from the unrelenting grief.

There is not space here to recount all of his cruelties, both stark and grim and creepingly nuanced, that led to me – a bold, buoyant, bright-souled woman – feeling so low that I spent hours in bathrooms craving blankness. Instead, I'll share some of the lessons I learned; the valuable stock gleaned from years spent angrily boiling over a relationship that left me a carcass of myself.

I cannot impress this upon you strongly enough: make sure a person's words match their actions. 'I'm sorry.' 'I won't do that to you again.' 'I promise I will be there.' 'I would never hurt you on purpose.' 'I love you.' These statements mean nothing unless they are backed up by behaviour. Love is something you do, not just something you say. If they don't treat love like a verb, you *must* kick them to the kerb.

Frequently, when Number 35 mistreated me, he would blame mental health issues, and imply that if I left him I'd be selfishly abandoning a poor, sick man who needed my support to get well. I'd start out determined to walk away from the abuse, then he'd manipulate me into feeling that I was being more shallow than a paddling pool, and shame me into staying. Do not let your kindness become a weakness. If you don't draw a line, eventually you will drown.

After I finally escaped, and began a steep uphill haul of emotional, medical and financial healing, I became aware that my ex had gone on to desecrate at least two additional women's lives in similar ways. He was the git that kept on giving. It seemed he hadn't edited himself in any way: the lying, the cheating, the acidic erosion of self-confidence, the gaslighting . . . he was still performing all his greatest hits.

I was crushed that the suffering he'd put me through hadn't changed him. Knowing he was sufficiently remorseful not to repeat such atrocities with others would have been bittersweet balm, but he didn't even grant me that. He didn't care enough to change when he was with me; he didn't care enough to change when I was gone.

But you must not depend upon the future actions of exes to bring retrospective value to your past experiences. Rely on them to bring you peace and closure, and you're still allowing them to dominate you.

You have to find your own truths and teachings. Sieve through that shit yourself to pan out the gold, then let the silt and slurry wash away. You'll move on richer for it.

Number 6

Standing before me naked, grinning, pale as the ghost of a veal calf and spattered with cinnamon freckles, Number 6 addressed the elephant in the room: the fact that what he'd just unveiled was not of elephantine proportions.

'It's a bit thin, isn't it? But I'm willing to bet we'll both have fun with it,' he quipped. I didn't know how to respond; I think I gargled a few unintelligible yet enthusiastic vowel sounds. It was skinnier than other penises I'd seen, but then this quintessential lovable rogue had done the do with so many women, that I half suspected his slender proportions were the result of being gradually sanded down through repeated use.

In fact, he proved to me that the old adage is true: it's not what you've got, it's what you do with it. And your attitude towards it. Not only was the sex so terrific that my vagina performed multiple Mexican waves in celebration, but he was such good fun, and so relaxed and joyously accepting of his own body, that I didn't feel the need to hang on to my own hang-ups either.

It's infinitely easier said than done, but don't bemoan what you've got – own what you've got. As Number 6 showed me, the fewer fucks you give about what you look like in bed, the better the fucks you'll have.

Number 31

Number 31 purported to want to make my life plush, but he became a murderous pillow of a person; he was the lover who smothered.

At first I felt so spoiled by the extravagant gifts, the insistence on paying for dinners, the chivalry that stopped only a shade short of laying his coat over every puddle in my path. But after dipping my toes into this relationship for a few weeks, I discovered something sinister lurking beneath, threatening to drown my independence.

If I tried to protest that the presents really were too much, when I privately began to feel obligated to make commitments I wasn't ready for in return for this ostensible generosity, I was branded 'ungrateful'. When I expressed that it was important to me to support myself with my own cash, to choose and fund my own decisions, I was tersely told that I 'needed to learn to accept assistance with grace'. By presenting his every action as kind, helpful and benevolent, he made it ominously hard to say 'no' without feeling guilty. It was sugar-coated control. I began to dread the apparent courtesy of his opening every door to usher me through, because I got the distinct sensation that he was thinking about locking them behind me.

If what begins as 'looking after you' morphs into an infantilizing refusal of your doing anything for yourself; if 'sweet' favours start to feel force-fed; if an offer leaves you no option to decline . . . beware: this is 'suffocaring'.

Push the goddamn exit door yourself, and run right through it.

Number 10

Oh god. We'd been mates for aeons. Although I'd always admired his floral language which made other people's chat seem like wilting forecourt carnations – and his unfathomable ability to wear a floaty kimono and jeans without looking like an utter knobsatchel – that night the red wine shoved us both just hard enough to shunt friendship into sexual fascination.

Despite his beauty, he hadn't been touched in too long. The mood was intense; theatrical; promising poetry.

Showing off, I went down on him, taking him back deeply in my throat, looking him dead in the eye . . . and he came so hard within thirty seconds that ejaculate spurted up inside my nasal cavity and shot forcefully out of both my nostrils.

This is a thing that can happen. This is a devastatingly daft, excruciatingly slapstick, ego-exterminatingly funny thing that can happen.

So now you know. As does my nose.

LOVE IS SOMETHING YOU DO, NOT JUST SOMETHING YOU SAY.

ROXANE
GAY

LIFE LESSON NO.12
**EMBRACE YOUR OWN
AMBITION**

My ambition is insatiable. Every success I achieve inspires a desire – and sometimes a need – to achieve more. I used to be embarrassed by my ambition and the ferocity of it. It felt unseemly, particularly as a woman, to want so much, to be naked in my desire for success. At the same time, I know that whatever success I may have achieved is a direct result of my drive and how I'm always, always reaching for more.

I have long been ambitious and competitive. As a child these instincts were honed by my parents who demanded excellence from my brothers and I. Their expectation was that our only job, as children, was to go to school and because that was our only job, it was our responsibility to excel. Fortunately, I took to school and being the best student I could be. I took real pride in exceeding teachers' expectations. Report cards were not merely chronicles of my performance, they were evidence of the quality of the fruits of my young labour. Certainly, it was intense to live with so much pressure, and not for everyone I realize, but I thrived on it. I not only wanted to please my parents, I wanted to impress my teachers and classmates. I wanted to impress myself. And so I worked hard. I decided that perfection was the only option.

Many years later, I am no longer a child. The only person who demands excellence from me is, well, me. I recognize that perfection is neither a realistic nor a healthy goal and that I can be excellent without being perfect. And still, I strive for more, more, more. Some of my drive rises from ambition and some of my drive rises from a need to exceed the expectations this culture has for me both as a woman and as a black woman. Some of my drive rises from impostor syndrome and a nagging worry that sooner rather than later everyone who likes my writing will realize that I am not at all worthy of their attention.

But I try not to let the darker side of my ambition control me. I try to focus on the joys of success. I remind myself to not take anything I achieve for granted. And though I am incredibly ambitious, I am not so ambitious that success is the only measure of my happiness.

I am a writer and most of the time, when people talk about writing, they talk about the love of writing. Anything creative is, more often than not, a passionate pursuit rather than a realistic pursuit. Let me be clear – I love writing. It is one of my favourite ways to pass the time. The act of telling stories brings me a deep and genuine pleasure. I love being able to remake the world, or convey how I understand and move through the world, with words.

Writing is a sublime pleasure, but I have always taken myself seriously as a writer. As a child hunched over my typewriter, or in high school when I wrote the most melodramatic stories you could imagine, or in my twenties when I played the part of the deeply tormented writer, chain smoking in the dark of night as I sat at my computer, I took myself seriously. Writing has never been an indulgence. It is not a hobby. Writing has always been and is as much part of my life as breathing.

Part of taking myself seriously as a writer has been allowing myself to be ambitious as a writer. Even when I didn't know better, in my late teens and early twenties, I was submitting work to *The Paris Review* and *The New Yorker* – holy grails for a writer. I didn't think about how slim my chances were. Quite frankly, I did not realize how slim my chances were.

**" AND THOUGH I
AM INCREDIBLY
AMBITIOUS,
I AM NOT SO
AMBITIOUS THAT
SUCCESS IS THE
ONLY MEASURE OF
MY HAPPINESS.**

Instead, I thought about the excellence those magazines represented, how much I enjoyed reading them, and how I wanted to be good enough to be part of that excellence. I was rejected by those publications, and countless others, time and again but I was relentless. There were days when I received a rejection and immediately sent a new story to that same publication.

Of course, I don't recommend that tactic because it tends to irritate editors, but when I didn't know better, all I thought was, if a given editor didn't like the story I sent, surely they would like something else I've written. I always had something new to send because I was always writing. If anything, rejection provided a great deal of inspiration. 'I'll show them how much better I can write,' I would tell myself. (This is something I still tell myself when I encounter rejection.) Every rejection became another opportunity for me to try again. When rejections came with feedback, I read that feedback several times and then, once I got over my feelings (rage, bitterness, sorrow, what have you), I revised my work because more often than not, the feedback I received was thoughtful and in the best interest of my work. Sometimes, when I submitted that revised work, it met with acceptance and those acceptances were the most satisfying because they were hard-earned. They offered professional redemption. They allowed me to believe that I was, indeed, good enough to be a writer.

People, and women in particular, often ask me for advice on either how to make it as a writer or as whatever they are passionate about. I tell them to be committed, because half-hearted efforts will get them nowhere, to take themselves seriously even if no one else will, to be undeterred in the face of rejection or setback, to be always willing to learn, to know how to take constructive criticism and to know when not to take criticism, to believe in the value of what they have to offer, to be relentless. This last thing, I stress the most. Wilful persistence is critical to any kind of success. I also tell these women to embrace their ambition, and to do so openly, vigorously, joyfully. Though external validation has always helped keep the fire of my ambition stoked, I have never looked to anyone for permission to be ambitious, to be open about what I want for my career, for myself. Embracing my ambition has been one of the greatest gifts I have ever given myself.

WILFUL PERSISTENCE IS CRITICAL TO ANY KIND OF SUCCESS.

HANNAH AZIEB POOL

LIFE LESSON NO.13
NO ONE HAS THE RIGHT TO TOUCH YOUR HAIR

The first time I remember it happening is in the playground of my primary school in south Manchester, in the late 1980s. Small, sticky, pinky-white hands shooting out at an alarming pace, right towards my head. Blissfully naive, I stand there, wondering what they are reaching for. A bit of fluff on my shoulder, or maybe a fly from my face? I watch with curiosity as the hand moves closer, and then freeze with shock as it lands with a dull thump right in the middle of my afro. 'Can I touch your hair?' asks the owner of the hand, about five seconds too late.

My childhood is filled with such memories. So are my teens, my twenties, my thirties, in fact every decade, every year, most months, many weeks and far, far too many days. Details may vary – the location, the season, the number of wrinkles, but the routine is always the same. The hand, or rather its owner, is always white. Women seem to do it more than men (roughly 70:30 – I'm guessing most decent men are a little wary of randomly touching women), and by the time they ask (if they bother at all) it's too late, because they already are rummaging in my hair.

The struggles black women go through with our hair, or rather, with other people's desire to constantly touch it, judge it and tell us what to do with it, are nothing new. India Arie sang about it with 'I Am Not My Hair' (2006), a whole decade before Solange did it with her 2016 hit 'Don't Touch My Hair'.

For centuries, black women have been told by white society that our hair in its natural state isn't good enough.

It's no coincidence that the first self-made female American millionaire is considered to be Madam CJ Walker, daughter of slaves, who made her fortune selling hair and beauty products to black women in the 1900s.

Hair, like skin, gives us an insight into who is considered the most beautiful, and with hair, as with skin, the lighter – the closer to 'the white beauty ideal' – the better. Why does it matter? Because it's about power, and those who are the gatekeepers of what, or who, is considered the most beautiful, are those with the most power. And yes, of course there are plenty of white women whose hair is also not considered beautiful, who feel intense pressure to straighten, dye or alter their hair in some way. And I know that can be a burden. But whatever hair traumas a brunette with curly hair has, she is still a white woman, and as such is still far closer to the mainstream beauty ideal than any black woman will ever be. She will see herself reflected as the lead in films, she will regularly see herself represented on the cover of magazines, she will be able to walk up to any beauty counter and buy foundation that matches her skin tone. No matter how much I doctor my hair, the rest of me will never conform to the mainstream beauty standard.

Now that we've got that out of the way, allow me to let you into a secret: I love being a black woman. I love it so much I often wonder whether those who are not black women subconsciously realize how great it can be, and that is why they spend so much time trying to make us feel terrible about ourselves.

But while having to constantly defend my hair from wandering hands may not sound like that much of a big deal, it serves as a near daily reminder of the way in which black women are still seen by many as something to be played with, petted like a zoo animal, rather than treated as equals.

Learning to say 'no' to the question 'Can I touch your hair?' took years, but when I did finally manage it, it taught me valuable lessons about standing up for myself, and what happens when race, beauty and power collide.

As a young girl, growing up in Manchester, I would spend Sunday afternoons with a blue towel on my head, pretending it was my hair. I'd waste hours practicing flipping my 'hair' back and forth, squinting my eyes as I looked in the mirror, trying to imagine what I'd look like with long blonde locks. In my teens, I'd spend large chunks of pocket money on giant tubs of 'strong hold' gel, saturate my hair with it, scrape it back, secure it with a scrunchie (it was the late 80s) and hope for the best. The overall effect was not unlike a lopsided pineapple, as my 'friends' liked to point out. My attempts at a fringe were even less successful. I'd wet a section of my hair at the front, apply yet more gel (VO5, you're welcome) and try everything from sleeping with pencils in my hair, to walking around with plastic comb slides or anything else I thought might stretch my curls into submission overnight. At best I'd have a crispy fringe which stuck out more than it hung down. When nothing worked, I begged my dad to let me chemically straighten my hair, but he refused – he'd seen too many of his black female friends lose their hair for this exact reason. So I told him he was ruining my life and went back to my bedroom to practice my Janet Jackson moves.

For years I hated my hair. Hated that it grew up, not down, like that of my classmates. Hated that I couldn't have a proper ponytail that swished side to side during netball practice. I just wanted 'normal' hair that hung past my shoulders – ideally blonde, but I'd settle for black, brown, red. I didn't have a religious upbringing, so instead I prayed to the gods of beauty for 'white girl hair', just in case any of them were listening. Looking back, what upsets me most isn't how much

I wanted 'white girl' hair, it's how much time I spent hating my own, and by definition, myself.

Every time someone asks to touch my hair, I am reminded that my hair is 'not normal', it's considered 'different', 'exotic' and doesn't belong, and by extension, neither do I. Asking to touch someone's hair is a classic case of what is known as 'othering' – treating the person as 'not one of us', seeing them as a 'thing' and alien, rather than a person.

'Can I touch your hair?' might seem like a harmless question, but it's usually code for 'you're not white'. It's not the question itself that's the problem, it's the context, the fact it's always one type of person (white) asking it to another (black) and the fact black people get it all the time. It's what is known as a 'racial microaggression'. These are the seemingly small, often brief, but continual race-based insults, degradations and humiliations black people have to deal with every single day. Everyday racism. Racism by a thousand cuts.

There aren't the big bad words that even the biggest of bigots are wary of using in polite society, but those subtle phrases and seemingly innocuous questions that form the white noise of life for many black women – and men – living in a white society. It's the stupid, often-repeated things people say and do to those they identify as being 'other'. They are subtle assertions of power to make sure you know your place and that you are most definitely not equal. It's being instantly followed around the store, it's constantly being asked 'where are you really from?' It's being told 'you don't sound black' (does black have a sound?). If it's something that white people do, or say, on a regular basis, to black people, but that white people don't really think is a big deal, chances are it's a microaggression. Only black people are constantly asked 'Can I touch your hair?', because only black people's hair is assumed to be not 'normal'.

TELLING ME MY HAIR IS SOFT IS NOT A COMPLIMENT. IT JUST SHOWS HOW WEIRD YOUR VIEWS ABOUT BLACK PEOPLE ARE.

People have generally stopped rubbing my skin to see if the black comes off, or being surprised my blood is the same colour as theirs, so why is there still the desire to touch my hair, and why the shock when it turns out that my hair feels, well, just like hair? Telling me my hair is soft, when you expected it to be coarse, is not a compliment; it just shows how weird your views about black people are. I am not your pet. I am not your plaything. My hair is not asking for your approval. My hair is not here for your education or amusement. We may be friends, we may be colleagues, but unless you are my hairdresser, or my lover (and even then, approach with caution), then please, do not touch my hair.

KATIE PIPER

LIFE LESSON NO.14
**ANYONE CAN LEARN
TO BE CONFIDENT**

For most of my life I was someone who envied other women's confidence. I'd see someone walk into a party and own the room – all statement hair and outlandish, creative outfits – while I'd be standing in a corner, wondering how I'd ended up here in the first place. I'd watch girls stand on stage talking so articulately, so *intelligently*, that I'd find myself staring in awe, pulling apart their hand gestures and their body language, trying to work out what they were doing; what they had that I didn't have; how unfair it was that I wasn't like them.

Then, one day, a couple of years ago, I realized that I *could* be like them, if I wanted to. I could also walk into a room with my shoulders back and my chin high, if I wanted to. I could stand on a stage, and speak clearly, without stumbling. I could pretend to be a confident person, and confidence would come to me. Because confidence isn't an exclusive club that you're born into. Confidence is just a state of mind. It's the behavioural equivalent of the Emperor's New Clothes: walk the walk, and everyone will hear you talking the talk. If you act like you belong, then everyone will think you do. In the same way that if you smile you project happiness – and then feel your mood lift at the same time – if you stand up straight and lean forward and make out like you're the kind of person who knows what she's doing, then those around you will think you really do. For me, it took a little bit of practice – reminding myself 'you can do this'. But over time, it becomes more natural.

So yes, confidence is a choice. But that doesn't mean it doesn't take work. In the same way that we go to the gym to develop our physical strength, and just as we complete daily sessions of mindfulness to boost our mental health, I've learned that feeling self-assured requires a certain form of daily practice too. Pushing myself to start conversations with people I previously assumed were too important to talk to me. Forcing myself to share my thoughts, rather than swallowing them down because I thought I wasn't qualified. I learned that reading helps me to feel like my opinions are valid, so that when I voice them, I can hear the conviction – the confidence – in my own voice. In a way, confidence feels like a muscle to me: the more you work on it, the stronger it will become. And – to continue the gym analogy – if you can build up your core, then it doesn't matter what the world throws at you. You'll always have the inner mettle to see you through.

A lot of things have happened to me in my life – some of which, like the birth of my daughter and the success of my career, have built me up to be taller and prouder of myself than I ever could have imagined. And then there have been other things, like the weeks and months after I was attacked, which have threatened to break my spirit altogether. But I'm endlessly grateful to my mum, Diane, for instilling a fundamental sense of confidence in me throughout my childhood. The reassuring knowledge that she was always there – a quiet constant in the background – gave me the freedom to try new things and take bigger risks when I was growing up, and then carry those lessons forward as an adult. After all, what's the worst that can happen when your mum is always there to pick you up when you fall? Sometimes I think that my underlying conviction that 'things will work out OK' is entirely down to her. You can't just tell people to 'be confident' – it's like telling someone to keep their chin up and expecting them to suddenly feel euphoric. But you can be there for another person, consistently and unwaveringly. And you can see how that bolsters their self-worth.

In my case, my mum's presence taught me to throw myself into things 100 per cent, then work out the fiddly details later. Judo, horse riding, Brownies . . . I'd try anything. And trying new activities helped me confront my own weaknesses and realize that if you work hard enough at something – even if you've never done it before – your proficiency and confidence will naturally grow. It doesn't matter if it's public speaking or horse riding – practice makes progress, and progress makes you feel really, *really* good. Every Saturday when I was growing up, I'd make my mum drive me to the nearest stables so that I could learn to jump and canter and gallop around a field. I was completely fearless and I worked hard at improving. I'd leap from the pony at the end of each session, desperate to tell my mum about how awesome I'd been; listing everything amazing thing I'd done in a breathless stream of confidence and excitement. Sometimes I miss that feeling – as women, I think we're often ashamed to own the things we've worked hard to attain. These days when I feel intimidated, I try to remember the confidence I had when I was twelve.

My surgeon once told me to only worry about tomorrow when tomorrow arrives, because worrying is just a waste of time. I've always thought that it was good advice – he's a very wise man, my surgeon – but sometimes I still forget it. Last year, I agreed to take part in a live catwalk show. Those of us appearing were supposed to be wearing outfits that represented the happiest moments of our lives – so I chose my wedding dress. But I'd been running around in the weeks leading up to the event and had forgotten to try it on until the night before. As my husband tried and failed to do up the zip, I found myself panicking. I was suddenly so self-conscious – all these people were going to be looking at me, judging me for not fitting into a dress that was only a year old – and there wasn't time to fix it. It was only when I took the time to try and look at the bigger picture – remembering that the event was about happy memories, not perfectly toned bodies – that I managed to calm down. It's so easy to think everyone is staring at you and critiquing you in their heads, but in reality, people are busy worrying about themselves and don't pay as much attention as you'd think. When I wore the dress the next day – tied on with a piece of string – I felt amazing.

My surgeon made a good point, but he forgot one thing. As well as not worrying about tomorrow, it's important not to focus on yesterday either. In my case, I don't want to think about my attack any more. Most people know my story – and I'm not ashamed of it, at all. But a lot of my confidence is directly tied to looking forward, rather than back, and sometimes I wish people would let me move on from that part of my story. Of course, my sense of worth was reshaped by that time in my life. Learning to feel confident again was often a matter of taking ten steps forward, and then nine steps back. But whenever you look at the past, the things that knock your confidence the most always seem insurmountably huge at the time – and then, with patience and hard work, you can put them in perspective and find your confidence again. Just think about when you were little and the biggest thing you had to deal with was a falling out with a friend. You'd be best mates again by the next lunchtime, but you'd still spend the hours in between crying into your school uniform sleeves because you thought your life was over. I get so many messages from young girls asking me for advice. All I ever want to say is 'don't sweat the small stuff'. Work hard and follow your instincts, and you'll be alright.

That said, the small stuff is pretty important sometimes. There are lots of different kinds of confidence. There's the confidence that comes from working really hard for something, then seeing it come together. There's the slow-build, core confidence that I think originates from stability and support. And then there's momentary, fleeting confidence, which maybe comes from the way we look or the clothes we wear. Sure, that temporary boost of 'I look great today' might not keep you in a job or sustain a happy, balanced marriage, but it can make you feel amazing – and feeling amazing is really important. Find the little things that give you a confidence boost, and make time for them. In my case, that involves persuading my husband to give me a spray tan once a week (he has a painting and decorating qualification, so he's really good at it) and it involves reading, too. A few years ago I discovered that the more I learn, the more confident I feel. So I take time to read whenever I can – scribbling down quotes I like on Post-it notes and sticking them on my bathroom mirror. My favourite one at the moment is 'anxiety is a waste of time – all it does is keep you very busy doing nothing at all'. As someone who worries constantly, it struck a chord.

And here's the secret: once you learn that confidence is there for the taking, you start to realize that sometimes, the people who seem the most self-assured probably aren't. The people who wear the loudest clothes, or have the boldest hairstyles, might just be using fashion as a costume to help them out of their shell. The people who talk loudly and dominate conversations, might just be doing so because they're nervous about not being respected enough. And the people who stand there quietly in the corner, might just be the ones who end up feeling the most confident of all.

MY OLD FACE

A POEM BY KATIE PIPER

I miss you

I think about you every day

The fun we used to have, those memories I have of you,
I will always treasure.

I know, I know you are gone forever – but never forgotten
We were crazy together and I am glad, we really made
the most of it.

I find it hard to think about the fact you don't exist in
this world any more.

So strange

Sometimes I wonder if we will be reunited in heaven?

I took care of you, all those expensive creams, if I close my eyes I can picture and feel all the contours as I would rub the face cream on, the flat wide nose, the perfect cupid's bow. I spent so much time perfecting those unruly brows!

I'm sorry I sometimes put you through the sunbed, that horrifies me now!

You'd be shocked, I've really changed. I'm kind to this face and I love it, but nothing will replace you. Sometimes I'm too hard on this face. If I had one wish I would see you again, for one day, wear you again, I would take you to the supermarket and walk you around, smiling, greeting everyone.

I'm sorry I let you down and let him take you away.

I will never destroy your pictures. I'm scared as you fade in my mind and I accept this face more. But I'm sorry it's the way it must be until we meet again.

NINA
STIBBE

LIFE LESSON NO.15
**WHY 99% OF ADVICE
CAN BE IGNORED**

When I was a child people were always dishing out advice. If a neighbour saw you mowing the lawn, they'd wander over and give you a tip. Sometimes it would be reasonable. Sometimes it'd be no more than a vague thought, and on a bad day it would be the type of advice that contradicts commonly held beliefs.

Some advice, like that from my granny, wasn't meant for anyone in particular but came from some strange moment in her own history (never trust a man who drives in a hat). Some wasn't advice so much as superstition (never cross on the stairs or you'll never marry). There was deliberately bad advice that siblings might give each other for entertainment (touch that electric fence, it won't hurt). And my mother's equally bad but well-meant (just tell the teacher how you feel) type advice, which never quite worked because she lived in a dream world in which teachers were nice.

As I grew up I was able tell these different types of advice apart. I stopped respecting all advice equally, and believing that giving advice was in itself a sign of wisdom.

Nowadays, as a writer in my fifties, I'm often asked what advice I'd give to budding writers. The short answer is: read a lot and write a lot. Also, if there's time, I might mention that although I've been writing all my life, I got my first book contract at the age of fifty, and I might well add that it was taking advice that caused the delay!

I peaked intellectually around the age of ten and my writing style was at its best back then. I wrote naturally, from experience, about real people – my mother, my sister and brothers, Princess Anne and various neighbours. Occasionally I might give them imaginary things to do but I never had them flying in the air or going back in time. I only had them falling in love or out of a window, things they might actually do.

I felt all set for a writer's life. In fact, positive feedback from my first few teachers at junior school caused me to give up on early dreams of becoming a lady jockey. I reckoned I was as good a writer as rider, if not better, plus I'd heard about lady jockeys being only allowed to eat lettuce leaves and diet biscuits – and that sounded too grim.

My writing confidence took a knock however when a new teacher, I'll call her 'Miss Long', gave me a mediocre review for my true-life story about the dangers of men who drove wearing hats. Any writer knows that a mediocre review is almost worse than a bad review because you can't pass it off as a grudge! Not only did Miss Long give me a mediocre review but she also gave me two pieces of advice:

Firstly, I should not use the same word twice – if I wanted to reiterate that sunlight was shimmering on the lake I should find a different word. I took that on board, but put it down to her being teacher-y. The second bit of advice was more serious. She said I'd tell a better story if I was more imaginative – here she used the example of my friend's fantastical tale about a flying chair that took her back to the Stone Age. I politely told Miss Long that real life was a strange, magical adventure and just as exciting as talking pigs, flying chairs and Stone Age barbecues.

But even though I disagreed completely, Miss Long's advice lodged itself in my mind and what followed was forty-odd years of trying too hard, forcing my writing, doing things that didn't feel right and searching in the thesaurus for different words.

By now I'd touched an electric fence and worn peach and purple dungarees that apparently suited me for a whole summer, but advice-about-writing proved harder to ignore, possibly because I wasn't successful at it and hadn't been published, and therefore felt I must be doing it wrong, and when the person giving the advice is successful – which they must be or how are you reading it? – they must be right. Also, it's not a fence, a lawn or dungarees you're dealing with – it's your heart and soul.

I read that a good writer would never use any verb except 'said' to carry speech. A good writer would never write 'then this' or 'then that' or 'all of a sudden' or 'before I knew it'. They wouldn't write about the weather and definitely not heat waves or storms brewing. A proper writer wouldn't write that someone was mean; they'd *show* them being mean (don't tell, show!). The thing was, as a reader, I quite liked being shown *and* told. I read that no one wants to read vivid descriptions of a person's appearance.

I noticed a famous author assert that: 'No writer worth his salt uses the first-person narrative.' I read things like: 'A satisfying story must have multiple strands, moving simultaneously forward, interweaving and coming together in resolution at the end.' And had to ask a friend what this meant. 'Like a really good episode of *Coronation Street*,' she said.

"

I NO LONGER HANG ON EVERY WORD OF THE OVERLY OPINIONATED GURU – THE 'DO' OR 'DON'T' OR 'ALWAYS' OR 'NEVER' TYPE OF ADVICE.

The rules and conventions began to almost overwhelm me but I battled on. My writing was soon at quite a distance from myself and although it felt unnatural, I assumed I must be on the right track. I started writing strange fiction told from someone else's point of view. My stories became convoluted and over-worked. I never quite pulled off the 'interweaving' and just when I started to wonder if I could actually be bothered with becoming a writer any more – and thought I might just go back to the lady-jockey plan and live on lettuce leaves – I heard this from a script-writing guru:

'Forget the rules! Do things your way – break with convention, tell your story backwards, give your story a quirky narrator!' and so on and so forth.

Being told to 'throw away the rule book' should have come as a relief but to be honest I felt all at sea and didn't know what to think.

I continued working on various different projects and from time to time I'd show my work to a friend and the odd literary agent. The friends were always kind but unconvincing and a couple of agents replied with encouraging rejections, but none of them jumped into a taxi with a contract and an ink pen.

Then suddenly (this is the important bit) at the age of fifty, after a publisher accidentally saw some of my work, I became a published author. The work of mine that caught her attention was something that I'd forgotten I'd even written. It WASN'T the multi-stranded wartime fiction (told in the third-person). Neither was it my intense mid-century family saga (in which only extraordinary things happened and I never used the same word twice). It wasn't even my unsettling told-backwards story in which I'd thrown convention to the wall and had it narrated by twins, both at the same time, infuriatingly.

This 'work' was never intended for publication at all. It was a collection of carelessly written letters that I'd sent to my sister almost thirty years previously when, aged twenty, I'd left home and become a nanny in London.

I'd missed chatting with my sister and almost every night I scribbled down the everyday goings-on of the household. Actually, my new life did feature some truly amazing things – the street where we lived was awash with talented and well-known writers, actors, artists and national treasures, many of whom were friendly with my boss – but I didn't bother writing much about any of them. I wrote the things I'd have told her had we still been sharing a bedroom – and in my own everyday voice.

I didn't write anything profound or philosophical, I wasn't trying to be funny or even particularly interesting. I wrote about people's haircuts, cardigans, chairs, how bad everyone was at making tea, disappointment with my new shoes and my boss's terrible eyeliner. The style of my writing was ordinary too. Apart from one or two actual poems, I made no effort to write poetically, grammatically or with any style, structure, or flow. I swore quite severely, called Shakespeare boring and described Thomas Hardy as a misery with a pea-shaped head.

I added scruffy pencil sketches in the margins too. Again, these were ordinary things: the chairs, the mysterious herbs my boss liked (basil), a new style of milk bottle, Gordon Banks the footballer and my new (disappointing) shoes.

Once I'd got my contract I assumed I'd be asked to tidy up the story or tweak things a bit to help the narrative flow. I thought I might have to edit the language, remove some of the cursing, or to explain things more clearly, or at least to erase the duplications of adjectives and verbs. But no, my editor wanted them exactly as I'd written them. What was important was authenticity of voice. This kind of writing didn't have to seem real or purposeful. It was real and purposeful.

So, my advice to budding writers is don't take advice that doesn't feel right for you. At least try writing in your own voice and in a way that feels natural.

After years of trying too hard (I suspect many of us fall into this trap – and not only in our writing) I now know that my simple style is OK and my ordinary voice is strong enough to carry a story. Also, the confidence I had at ten years old has returned and I'm happy to write the same word twice – and I still believe that real life is a strange, magical adventure and just as exciting as talking pigs, flying chairs and Stone Age barbecues. I now only take notice of general advice – offering tips, tricks and ideas on motivation and creativity. I've learned that advice from real friends is often better than detailed advice from experts. I no longer hang on every word of the overly opinionated guru – the DO or DON'T or ALWAYS or NEVER type of advice. And I've come to the conclusion that unless the advice-giver actually knows you and your work it's unlikely they will know with any certainty what's best for you. Sure, I listen to advice from my editor, my agent, my sister and my friend Stella, but crucially – these days it feels like I might actually know best.

ANNA
FIELDING

LIFE LESSON NO.16
**ELEVEN STORIES
ABOUT GRIEF**

Three months ago my father died. A year and a half before that, my grandfather died. Months before that, my paternal grandmother, Dorothy, and my boyfriend's stepmother died.

A year before that, my Uncle Bob. Within far too recent memory, I have also lost my Aunt Jane; my Uncle Pete; my maternal grandmother, Beryl; my cherished great aunt; a university friend and an ex-boyfriend. Even though I am at an age where many people marry, during this time I have worn black to ceremonies more often than I have worn florals.

I have four different eulogies saved in Pages for iPad.

I'm still not sure I know what grief is.

What we all know is that grief is terrible and destabilizing. If I had only read the paragraphs above, rather than writing them, I would assume the author was weeping in the rain, rending her hair. The whole gothic drama. Perhaps slightly modernized, expecting to read something confessional, where loss is subsumed in drink and drugs and cigarettes and terrible sex.

But it isn't like that, is it? I hate listing everyone and then making it about the impact on me, me, me. They all deserve a whole book each. I have not included some names, out of respect for the living, because of other people who cared and loved and are missing someone more. Because we are talking about grieving, and not about the dead. I do know that grieving is what the living deal with and I was still unprepared for how it would take me. How painful, yes, but how mundane, how ridiculous, how beautiful and loving. I'm too near to have an over-arching theory, especially so close to my dad.

My experiences will not be universal. These are small stories, because I'm not out of the woods, yet. But here are my markers on trees for anyone else who's lost too.

Sometimes I wonder if it's easier for the dying

It's late February and my dad is in hospital for the last time. It's been a long illness and he has been in and out of the Princess Royal for over two years. I have been up to Shropshire and back down to London with increasing frequency. Hospital parking vouchers flutter from my stepmother's purse and in the dip near the gear stick in her car.

At first, and entirely in character, Dad didn't seem to be taking things very seriously, at least on the surface. He would strap on his nebulizer mask and pretend to be a Spitfire pilot in an old war film. He threw a huge barbecue for his seventy-first birthday, cheerfully telling everyone they had to come because it would be his last (he turned seventy-two a year later). 'Oh woe! Woe!' he would say in melodramatic tones. 'What will you do without me?'

My father was an individual. And occasionally a bit of a pain.

But I also take refuge in flippancy and getting a laugh, so sometimes it was fun to play along and enjoy the two of us being silly together (I did a pretty decent 1930s radio operator to go with his pilot). Sometimes I would smile the best I could and try not to meet my stepmother's eyes.

On Christmas Day, just before everyone arrived for dinner, we sat in the living room. I was wearing a party frock to give the day a sense of occasion, plus yellow rubber gloves and a pinafore apron.

'An interesting outfit, daughter dear,' he said. His chest crackled on the in-breath. 'Are the gloves all the fashion down in that London?'

I gave him a look. 'It's festive,' I said in a teenage-sulk tone.

Another crackle as we both breathed in the Christmas dinner cooking smells. 'This will be my last one,' he said, serious for once. 'Come on, bab, no tears. I've lived my life exactly as I've wanted to. I wouldn't change it. It's no bad thing to be able to say that.'

In the hospital, in that last week, I sit by the bed with Corrine, my stepmother, holding hands, crying silently. I rub lotion into Dad's feet, which look dry. I sit with my uncle, as he contemplates being the only one left of four brothers. I watch Dad become more peaceful, as the hospital finally work out the right combination of painkillers. The man in the next bed has a kind face and an old-fashioned Shropshire burr. 'He's not been so restless,' he says. 'He bin sleepin.' His kindness is for me and Corrine, not concern for Dad, not now. There is morphine and there is acceptance.

Away from the bed, our brains are muddy and our heartbeats disturbed.

Just after 6 a.m., 28 February 2017

My stepmother knocks on the bedroom door. 'Anna?' Neither of us have been sleeping well. I know from her voice, and the time of day. There's a moment of blankness. I can hear the river at the bottom of the garden, running fast and high with the winter rain.

We cry, then rush to dress. But my dad has already died in the night. And we weren't there.

9 THINGS I COULD NOT DO IN THE FIRST TWO WEEKS

1. Focus properly, on anything.

2. Be patient with the dog.

3. Stop my stomach churning. Extreme emotions always make me throw up.

4. Read anything except magazines.

5. Control my weird, hysterical laughter when I realized the newsagent had five magazines about tractors, nine about fishing and only one fashion title, one that I'd already read. I walked out of the shop because everyone was looking.

6. Tell people, my boyfriend, my mum, my friends, how I actually felt. Because I didn't know.

7. Reply to texts, emails, WhatsApps from caring friends and cousins.

8. Adjust to the new tenses. 'My dad is . . .' I'd say. 'Dad and Corrine live in . .'. Correcting myself hurt a lot. It still does.

9. Stop sitting on the bed and staring at the River Severn, thinking that it had carried on flowing through so many lifetimes. Sometimes this was comforting, sometimes I resented it for being so old. The bloody, bastard, indifferent river.

Transferable skills

'What font will it be in?' I said to the undertaker, about the death notice in the local paper.

'I can honestly say no one's ever asked me that before,' she said.

My dad and my stepmother used to run a pub. Corrine knows immediately how many people a side of salmon will feed at a buffet, can estimate how many wine glasses will be needed at a wake. I had no idea, but as a journalist, I could plan an order of service, with a pleasing layout over the right number of pages. I sent the printers lengthy, picky emails about what text should be in italics and what pictures needed to be made lighter. I wrote, too, anything that needed writing.

It feels so good to know there's something of you left. That amid the numbness and the sadness, there are still things that you have learned, still skills you can use. Maybe one day, all the other parts of you, the parts that have been shocked into retreat, will come back too.

'They said you were very thorough,' said the undertaker of the printers.

I have a feeling she was being tactful.

What about me?

Flowers. Flowers. Early spring flowers, everywhere. As many cards as Christmas. Knocks on the door from neighbours with dogs, neighbours with cards, friends with flowers, all with sympathy, nearly all for my stepmother. In the language of florists' cards I am 'and family'.

Look, look, I know. I have a phone full of electronic messages, so many that I'm almost shocked by the loveliness of my friends. My mum comes. My boyfriend. I know my stepmother has lost the man she built her life with. And I am living, temporarily, geographically, right in the middle of her support system. I don't begrudge. I'm really, truly glad for her. But there's a small howl inside me when the undertaker introduces Corrine to a colleague, not me. When the post comes, again, and again I'm 'and family'.

A card, and then another card, appear from Lorraine's handbag. She and her husband have been friends with Dad and Corrine for years, have known me since I was twelve. 'When my dad died everyone focused on my mum,' she says. 'I wanted to say, "I've lost my dad, too!"' I value this so much that I sleep with the card under my pillow. In the morning I put it back on the mantelpiece, so Corrine doesn't notice and feel bad for me.

Could you please fix the conservatory door?

During the period of planning the funeral, the handle fell off the door connecting the living room and the conservatory. We kept jamming it back on, then swearing when it fell off again. Emotions, including irritation, are close to the surface when you are planning a funeral.

People would come around and say, 'You must let me know if there's anything I can do.' And we'd say, 'There is, actually. The handle on the door to the conservatory keeps falling off. Could you have a go at fixing it?'

And people looked a bit taken aback that it was something so mundane. But your whole stupid, mundane life just carries on happening while you try to deal with everything else. During the month of March, four different people tried to fix the handle on the door to the conservatory. It is still broken.

As strange and beautiful as a wedding

The saddest funeral would be an empty one. I am lucky in that my father was both well known and well liked. The acceptable thing to say would be that this made the day easier. I have started to think we should all care less about what is acceptable and focus on what is truthful. So, truthfully, it made the day fun, in some parts. He would have liked that.

I felt disassociated at first, as though I'd wandered onto a film set populated with people I love, wearing the costumes, moving through the motions. My memories have formed in flashes. The crepe-viscose mix of my dress sliding against the leather of the funeral car upholstery as we take corners. My cousin William's white-blond hair against his dark suit. Walking through so many people, my boyfriend holding one hand and my cousin Becky the other, to the front of the crematorium. Standing to read what I wrote for him; wondering why the short walk to the lectern seems so far; wondering why my voice is shaking.

At one point a dark-haired woman approached. 'You don't know me,' she said. 'We had our wedding at your dad's pub. My dad got really nervous about the speech, too nervous to give it, so your dad stepped in instead! We're still married!' she gestured at the man beside her. 'He was part of our wedding, so we wanted to be here today.'

In truth, the day reminds me of a wedding. The marvelling feeling that 'This is us, dressed in these clothes, doing this thing.' The story swapping and the hugging and the bright-eyed tears. The old friends and re-acquaintances. It's an end, not a beginning, but the love is the same.

I'm glad he got to do a wedding speech for someone.

Collateral damage

After leaving my father's funeral, I tripped on a rug and smacked my mouth on a sofa bed. Three months later there is still a small lump in my lip.

Don't drink your feelings. Even if everyone else is.

This is ridiculous

'I miss everybody,' I say, sobbing in bed. And, somehow, for my dad this has taken the form of missing the places I associate with him, too. This sensible sentence is not what I actually say out loud, and so not what my boyfriend hears. Instead: 'I've followed Ironbridge Parish Council on Twitter!' I howl, with a fresh round of tears.

See a therapist

Once a week, I sit in a room with a woman called Rebecca and either verbally bludgeon her with an over-caffeinated stream of consciousness or clam up. On the clamming days I tell her that I'm better written down or in front of an audience. I'm not good at asking for help, I need someone to tease problems out of me. I have been a clam with my boyfriend. I have deflected my friends with jokes and not ever got to the point.

Perhaps you're better, perhaps you stick at different points. I've found that someone professional in the listening role, an hour in which it was more embarrassing to not talk than to talk, works for me. But talking has helped – and I think it helps all of us.

Just after 6 a.m., 18 June 2017

There is another river about 100 metres away, fed by churning burns, and brown with peat and mad with waterfalls. It's not my Severn, but it's just as hypnotic. I have escaped to western Scotland, green and remote, to do yoga, sit in a hot tub and try to unpick the jumble in my head.

It's also Father's Day.

There is little WiFi and no 4G. I am sparing myself your Instagrams of unwrapped golfing jumpers and meals in family homes, from the Facebook posts of male friends, grinning with their baby daughters and the first of a lifetime of cards.

Loss remakes you. I have my own series of firsts to go through now, and I won't be able to take evasive action for all of them. Last month I started wearing glasses: I cried and cried thinking my dad would never tease me about them and never even see me wear them. There will be new rivers, new glasses, new versions of me and I must get used to the gap where the person I would like to share them with is. I must get used to the new normal.

LOSS REMAKES YOU.

ROBYN WILDER

LIFE LESSON NO.17
YOU'RE NOT THE WORST MUM IN THE WORLD

Dear new, tired, overwhelmed mum,

Hello, my name is Robyn Wilder. I'm a mum, too – a bit further down the line from where you are. Two frozen Januarys ago, amid the early morning alarms of an induced labour gone awry, I gave birth to my son, Herbie, by emergency caesarean section. Four evenings later (I don't know what your hospital is like, but at mine they like to thrill you with rumours of discharging you at 8 a.m. before actually doing so past 10 p.m.) I went home to a dark, unheated house – with a tiny new scrap of life in my arms, and no idea what to do next.

I was supposed to feel joy and bliss. I was supposed to have a handle on when next to change the car-sized maternity pad between my legs. Instead I just felt panic. Enormous love, but also a suffocating panic that I suspect I'd have felt even if I'd sneezed the baby out and been carried home on an upholstered palanquin.

Because, as you know, it is a very strange thing to have a baby. It's a bit like bringing home a new kitten, only a kitten you have very many complicated feelings for, and one that changes your body, relationship, career and home, and makes it impossible to watch any psychological thriller involving children in peril.

Incidentally, don't worry if you have to put this book down to attend to your baby, or a cup of coffee that's still above room temperature, or to rewind that Netflix show that revealed the murderer just as your baby farted too loudly. I'll be here when you get back. And when you do get back, I'd like to talk to you about perfection.

Despite the fact that I'm the sort of person who gets lost within her own postcode, and regularly trips over great lumps of nothing in the street, I somehow expected to be a perfect parent. I'd read the manuals and decided what sort of parenting style I wanted to adopt ('gentle', with a touch of 'French', because they are stylish and drink wine). I assured my boss I'd be back at work within three months of giving birth. I draped my son's nursery in so much bunting it looked as though Pinterest had thrown up on it. In short, I treated parenting options as though they were muted colours on a Farrow & Ball swatch. Really, I should have expected my expectations of perfection to be as violently punctured as they were.

Pregnancy

I fully expected to glow throughout my pregnancy – all sunlit and mellow with really great hair, demurely cupping my belly in a series of nauseating floral smocks. Instead, I developed morning sickness so severe I had to be rehydrated at hospital twice a month. I also got gestational diabetes, anaemia, cankles, and in my third trimester I *cracked a rib*.

My hair was pretty lush, though.

Birth

I don't remember a lot about the birth apart from vomiting, asking for Diet Coke a lot, then passing out from blood loss on the operating table. It was only in the weeks afterwards, when (very unwanted) images of blood and broken babies kept flashing before my eyes, that I realized how much my labour had affected me. When you're pregnant, people scare you with tales of ripped perineums and show you images of swollen, purple, baby-stuffed vulvas, but no one talks much about the quiet horror that can mess you up after a traumatic birth. Yet it happens. Post-birth PTSD is a thing, and it's different from the baby blues. It took two midwives and a doctor to convince me, but I did recover with their medicine and counselling.

Breastfeeding and formula

That my son breastfed at all was entirely to his credit – he latched on pretty much while I was still passed out after my C-section, and it seemed rude not to continue (in fact we did so for more than two years). Many people congratulated me for not 'resorting' to formula, which made me a bit stabby. I *like* formula – it's made *for* babies, by *science*. While a milk intolerance prevented Herbie from trying it, any future babies are going to get a bottle of the fake stuff at night so I can sleep. Talking of which . . .

Sleep

Thanks to a traumatic birth and silent reflux, Herbie would only sleep in our arms. Not by our side on a cushion, or in the arctic white expanse of his moses basket. Just our arms. For the first purgatorial month of my baby's life, my husband and I worked two-hour shifts, twenty-four hours a day, until a kind midwife – noticing our permanently closed eyes and deathly pallor – told us, a little conspiratorially, about safe bed-sharing. For the next eighteen months, Herbie slept in our bed, in the crook of my arm, and dream-fed through the night. I got comments from all quarters – neither the consultant nor my in-laws were fans. Words like 'Oedipus' and 'rod for your own back' were thrown around, but I didn't care. I was getting upwards of five hours' sleep a night, and that is like gold to a new mum. Whatever your setup – safe bed-sharing, cot at the end of the bed, a dark nursery and baby monitor, everyone in hammocks – if everyone in your house is sleeping, no one's opinion but yours matters.

Maternity leave

My expectations of maternity leave: finally write that book, take up knitting, watch all of *The West Wing*, finish *1Q84* by Haruki Murakami, go to an embroidery class, take up yoga.

What I actually achieved during maternity leave: went up a dress size, discovered *Pretty Little Liars*, lost my Lidl virginity.

The house

Three types of people visited my house after the baby was born: the type who would run a finger along the mantelpiece and turn up their nose; the type who'd say, 'Oh, leave it! Your baby won't remember a bit of dust'; and the type who'd just barrel in and start vacuuming (they were my favourites). The truth is, Herbie – although giggly, chubby and delightful – was the sort of baby who needed constant entertaining, so I couldn't just put him down and get on with housework. That said, a perpetually dirty house got me down, so while for the most part I took everyone's advice and slept when he did, I'd use one of his daily naps to tidy and/or run the hoover round, just so *I* felt better about things.

Work

Daycare and commuting – that was my plan from three months into motherhood. But, when it came to it, it seemed impossible – Herbie was still too tiny, and I couldn't countenance being away from him. So I quit my job and took up freelancing. I'd write from the kitchen table while Herbie napped or played in his bouncer, and pitch and do edits on my phone, with one hand, while he breastfed. It wasn't the easiest job but, for me at least, it beat meetings about meetings.

Activities

I was always hot on Herbie being stimulated – to the point where I read him *The Lion, the Witch and the Wardrobe* during his first week of life and was genuinely a bit shocked he wasn't interested. Soon Instagram became a constant companion, and I'd compare myself unfavourably to all the other parents on there who seemed to not only have all their shit together, but also completed long lists of daily baby activities – all while looking *amazing*. I'd scroll through my feed of adorable tots engaged in planting seeds, reading (reading!), or 'messy play', and a slow trickle of fear would drip down my belly as I'd look over at my own son, who was banging a spoon on the floor and had only been out once that day, to Lidl. In moments like this, it was hard to shake the sense that I was failing.

What worked for me

Letting go of others' expectations was key. Just smiling and nodding when they had something to say, and getting on with my day. This was harder than I expected it to be, because I have always been an inveterate people-pleaser. But the point is, I only had one person to please: my son. So when I stopped listening to others and started listening to him, it all became clear.

He was only a tiny baby, so he still needed the comfort of his mother to sleep, and to feed. He – more so than the housework, at least for the short term – needed my attention; in fact, he thrived on it. That's why really the only activity he needed until he was crawling and curious about the outside world, was to play with the people who loved him. For the longest time, messy play completely confounded him, and spoon-banging really was the game of choice.

So I listened to my baby, and started taking care of him the way he wanted me to (and the way that was easiest on me), and today I have a happy, curious, loved and cheeky two-year-old who is constantly on the hunt for new information (his latest trick is asking 'what's that?' every three seconds and I have already run out of answers). He sleeps in his own bed, does not have rickets, is not Oedipal, no longer chomps down on my boob every night, isn't covered in filth, socializes well and hasn't, despite my best efforts, developed an unhealthy fixation with Lidl.

Obviously not all babies, or parents, are the same, so all, none or some of the above will apply to you. But here is one universal truth – there is no such thing as a perfect parent, so please don't worry too much about being one. You might as well worry about being a unicorn. When all else fails, listen to your baby, listen to your own needs and listen to your gut.

At the time of writing I am five months pregnant, so obviously I will read this and a) not remember writing any of it, and b) hopefully take my own advice. At the risk of sounding trite, the Instagram-age mum-adage is true: you really do got this, Mama. But first, have a nap and, like, eight biscuits.

Love from an old, tired, still overwhelmed but slightly less terrified mum x

WHAT I ACTUALLY ACHIEVED DURING MATERNITY LEAVE: WENT UP A DRESS SIZE, DISCOVERED *PRETTY LITTLE LIARS*, LOST MY LIDL VIRGINITY.

NICOLA
ADAMS OBE

LIFE LESSON NO.18

ONLY YOU SET THE
BAR FOR YOUR
GOALS

Success, to me, is kind of like a shape-shifter. It never looks the same way for very long – as soon as you've chased one dream, there's another one over the horizon. I know it sounds exhausting, but in a way, I think it's probably what keeps me going. I'm never willing to settle down, to pat myself on the back and say, 'I'm done now.' There's always something more to work towards. There's always something bigger to compete for. There's always something else to win. And if you can take that ambition on board and ignore anyone who tries to hold you back, then you'll achieve more than you ever dreamed of.

I guess I'm lucky, because I grew up around people who told me I could do anything. From my mother to my boxing coach, everyone went out of their way to reinforce the idea that I could aim for the sky and that they'd never hold me back. But still, it was always me who set the goal posts. They were just there to cheer me along – and you can never underestimate how important that is. Their support was invaluable even *before* I was in the ring – I had to fight to get to fight in the first place, not least because there were so few competitions when I was starting out. So one thing I've learned in my life is how important it is to encourage those around you, even if their dreams seem different to your own.

The first time I went boxing, I was twelve years old, and my mum had dropped me off at an after-school club in the gym because she wanted to go to aerobics and couldn't find a babysitter. I guess I was always kind of competitive, but the second I walked into the ring that day, I was completely hooked. I was the only girl in the room, but the coach went out of his way to make sure everyone knew gender didn't exist in the ring. 'There's only one rule in here,' he said. 'You listen to what I say. It doesn't matter if you're a boy or a girl – you're all going to be treated exactly the same.' That was the moment when I remember thinking, 'I'm going to like it here.'

I already knew a bit about the sport. My dad would watch reruns of Muhammad Ali fights on TV, and I'd see him strutting about with all these medals and just having so much *fun*. That quickly became the way I defined success: achieving absolutely everything possible and pushing every single boundary, but enjoying yourself at the same time. In my case, it took me about a year of enjoying myself before I started achieving anything. My coach sat my mum down one day and said that, actually, I was quite talented – and would I be interested in competing? By that point I'd been fighting boys my age for twelve months, so it never occurred to me that being a girl could be a problem. Nobody had ever let my gender hold me back so far, so I didn't either.

The more competitions I won, the bigger my ambitions became. Every day, my mum was taking me to coaching sessions and telling me I could achieve anything, and I internalized that. I'll be grateful to her for that for the rest of my life. When one day, someone asked me what my ultimate dream was, I said I wanted to be an Olympic champion. Women's boxing wasn't even an Olympic sport at the time – but I was convinced that somehow, someday, I'd find a way to stand on that podium with a gold medal. The more I spoke about it, the more I believed in my abilities to make it happen. It didn't matter if someone told me I was delusional, or that boxing was just a silly phase I'd grow out of soon enough, or – worst of all – that I should be playing tennis instead. I just laughed it off, and secretly vowed to prove them all wrong. Stubborn determination is a useful quality in sport, I think. But while I was so lucky to be surrounded by people who told me I could do anything, I began to understand that some people will always try to tear you down. The thing is, if you want to realize your dreams, you can't let yourself listen to them. After all, you're the only person who knows what you're capable of. And if you don't believe in yourself completely, then nobody else is going to do it on your behalf.

It's the same when it comes to winning. I never, ever, think about what will happen if I lose a fight. If you think about losing, then you've already lost. Of course, sometimes it happens – and in those cases, it really affects my mood for a good couple of days. I'm not really the best person at dealing with that! But you can't let it take over or affect your self-worth. Better to remember the last time you won a match or achieved something really awesome, then try to recreate that feeling. These days, if something goes wrong, I try to channel the moment I won my first Olympic gold medal. I went into that match *knowing* I was going to win it. The woman I was fighting had beaten me at the World Championships, and I just grinned at her, because I knew this was my revenge. Later, standing on the podium, and thinking, 'Oh my God, I've done the thing I've been dreaming about since I was twelve', was a high I'll never forget, although it took a long while to sink in at the time.

Of course, everyone needs a break sometimes. It's all very well dreaming big and giving your dreams your all, but rest days are the best days. After winning the Olympics, I took a few days off to just go clubbing with my friends and spend time with my family. When I'm training for a big fight, I have to make so many social sacrifices, like missing birthdays and weddings, and that's really hard on everybody. It's even harder if someone questions me and tries to persuade me to change my mind.

When you've spent your whole life working towards something, it's a weird feeling to tick it off the To Do list. But that doesn't have to be it. You're in charge of your own aspirations – nobody else can say 'enough now', only you. That's why I went back to training five or six days after the London Olympics – because I knew I wasn't done yet. I knew the target on my back the second time around would be even bigger. Women from all over the world were trying to beat me, specifically. But that kind of pressure only motivates me to push myself even further. The more you work for something, the better the reward. And the more people tell you that you can't do something, the more satisfying it feels to prove them wrong.

Sometimes, it's not other people warning me I'm reaching my limits. Sometimes it's me. But I've learned to harness that fear and use it as another means for motivation. When I was training for Rio, I tripped and tore some of the tendons in my ankle. Suddenly, there was a panic – what if I wasn't fit enough for the qualifiers? But just as I don't listen to people who say I'm not good enough, I have to ignore the little voice in my head, too. I have a lot of experience, and I trust my own abilities. And when I won that gold medal a few months later, it meant so much to me – because I was showing the whole world, and myself, what I was capable of.

Still, sometimes shifting your goal posts isn't enough: sometimes you need to pick them up and move them to a different pitch altogether. After Rio, I realized I had achieved everything that I ever wanted to achieve as an amateur, and I wanted to go pro instead – which means fighting on a professional level, and developing new skills. Before making the decision, I spoke to everyone I knew – friends, family and coaches – and I gave myself the freedom to think even bigger than ever before: what did I really want to achieve next? What would give me a high equal to that of standing on a podium in Brazil? I think asking yourself 'what next?' is really important. It's not like I have it written on a Post-it note or something, but it's something I come back to a lot. As soon as you don't know what you're aiming for, it's easy to feel lost.

And there's something to be said for the thrill of starting over. As a pro boxer, I'm now fighting for a completely different audience, and against completely different people. I no longer have the financial support that comes with amateur boxing, so it's up to me to fund my whole team, which is a whole new kind of pressure to take on. In a way, I'm suddenly a one-woman enterprise, and it's so exciting – I get to design my own costumes and pick the music that I fight to. The fight itself is a performance as well as a competition, and that's daunting and exhilarating, all at the same time. But it doesn't mean I'm not still pushing myself as far as I can go: I was a World Champion amateur, and now I need to be a World Champion pro, too. Maybe when I've done that, I'll star in a Hollywood blockbuster, or get a role in *Game of Thrones*. Your life and your ambitions are up to you. It doesn't matter if you have experience already, or none at all. It doesn't matter if you're a woman. And it doesn't matter if you're aiming to win a gold medal in a competition that doesn't even exist yet. Nobody should ever be allowed to hold you back – least of all yourself.

PANDORA
SYKES

LIFE LESSON NO.19
**THE IMPORTANCE OF
TRIVIAL PURSUITS**

Recently, I discovered make-up. I don't mean literally. Just that I never saw it as my 'thing'. Shoes? Jackets? My thing. But while I wouldn't leave the house without my Nars Creamy Concealer in Custard, I didn't give a shit about mascara. Couldn't tell you the difference between a BB or a CC. Never used a primer (still haven't, to be fair). And then, in one huge cliché, I hit a birthday milestone and felt this seismic shift *yank* through my body.

I bought some caffeine for my puffy under-eyes that could no longer be blamed on a pillow and its creases; plus a retinoid and some hyaluronic acid from The Ordinary. With a pipette, I began to layer on all three, as advised. I started wearing mascara, thickly coating my lashes as I remembered, pleasingly, how black mascara makes blue eyes appear bluer. I became closely attached to my Scholl pedi razor – transfixed, as the dry skin was sanded from my feet – and I've become nothing short of obsessed with James Read's Sleep Mask Tan. All these relatively new forms of titivation do something for my soul. Or the outer parts of it, at least.

I could say this all happened because I turned thirty. But mostly, I think it happened because of my sister. And her cancer.

The world tilts when someone you love is diagnosed with cancer. For the first week after I found out, reality seemed to curl at the edges. Things went on like normal, but it felt as though a small thread in my life had come loose and it was fraying, constantly fraying – and I didn't have a sewing kit to darn it up again. What I did have, of course, was make-up.

You might think that a looming disease would put an end to small rituals. I think I did once, too. But I soon realized that the superficial trimmings are never more relevant than they are when someone gets really, really sick. Maybe it's because with cancer, at least, the way you tell how sick they are is by their surface: bloated, pale, bald. The week after she was diagnosed with breast cancer, my sister started furiously Googling products for 'chemo skin'. In tandem with her bounty of Zelens, Tata Harper, Oski and Kate Somerville products, she found herself a selection of colourful, delicately printed turbans by Dee Di Vita. My siblings and I ordered a ruinously expensive but jaw-droppingly chic silk kimono from Olivia von Halle, so that she could 'receive' her guests when chemo left her too ill to leave the house. She may have been feeling shit, but her trimmings were nothing short of ritzy.

Emotionally laden words of course meant everything: letters, texts, emails. But it was the small, seemingly trivial, oh-so pretty or sweet-smelling tokens which became, quite literally, her daily balm. For years, as a fashion journalist, I'd espoused the sentiment that our surface area was connected to the soul. But I'd never really invested in the beauty side of it until my sister got ill. As she reached for shiny things to make her dull skin shinier, I found myself doing the same.

As I'd long argued, the ornamental is most valued when you're at your lowest ebb. But now I was hearing it from the horse's mouth. 'Presents really do help,' said my sister, authoritative even when significantly below par. 'I want all the scented candles and bunches of flowers you've got, thanks.' To be spoilt and to spoil your skin makes a life not currently worth luxuriating in feel temporarily luxurious. A spot of colour, on a grey day; a soothing oil on parched, thin skin. Recently, my sister bought herself a big, fat, brown bottle of expensive bath oil from Aesop. Distracted, she smashed all £56 worth on the floor. She immediately burst into tears and was taken aback when a fresh bottle was thrust into her hand. 'It's on us,' they said. Of course, they couldn't have known. But they knew enough. Enough to know she really needed that bottle of bath oil.

That same day, as we wandered around the shops between hospital appointments, we went into The White Company. With a flash of dark humour, she chortled as she told me that she was going to ask the shop assistants if they did 'a cancer discount'. I begged her not to tease them. 'They'll keel over if you ask them that!' I whispered. 'Not if I keel over first,' she shot back. We sniggered.

I may have only recently discovered beauty, but my defence of personal *passementerie* began way before my brave and brilliant sister grew a tumour. (If you want to put a pin in the exact date, you could say it was when my mother caught me adjusting my pyjamas in the mirror, so that they hung correctly on my hips, at the age of four.)

Fast forward twenty years and pyjama pedantries had grown into my job, of sorts. For two and a half years, I had a newspaper column called 'Wardrobe Mistress' in which I answered readers' questions. Ostensibly, the question they asked was: 'What should I wear?' The subtext I answered was always: 'How can I feel good?' To talk about clothes and make-up with women is rarely to talk about clothes and make-up. It is not to wave a shoe in her face and trill, 'Wedges are on trend for spring!' It is psychological. I responded to how they felt; not necessarily what they told me they wanted to wear. And I learned more about women in those few years than I have in the rest of my entire life.

Yet while I could always see the value in this alter-ego of mine, she often seemed to negate the other parts of me, as both a journalist and a woman. Even now in the twenty-first century, pejorative connotations of personal titivation are still very much present. Once upon a time, I wrote a piece about my anxiety. I got several book offers off the back of that piece. But I also got various tweets, disparaging my story, on the very basis of (a part of) my job. One read: 'Stick to "Wardrobe Mistress." Or go to Syria for a year . . . ' I'm going to take a punt and say that the rest of that sentence, hanging unfinished, would read: 'where you can experience *real* anxiety, that isn't to do with a creased skirt'. Perhaps, by dint of my being a white, young, middle-class woman (ergo, hugely privileged) such responses are not surprising. But I can't help but think such missives are exacerbated by the fact that, a lot of the time, I write about the superficial. How deep could I really be?

I no longer just write about clothes. I write about social media and cultural psychology and go on panels about consumer behaviour. I host a pop-culture podcast (on which there is no fashion at all), I interview celebrities. But still, when I go to a party, someone will introduce me as, 'Pandora – she will tell you what to wear!' and to a certain type of human – typically older, male – I automatically become a fashion-obsessed bimbo. A woman solely of surface. I watched it happen recently, at a party for a political magazine. I entered into conversation with a political journalist, whose hooded eyes dropped a fraction lower when the introduction was made. 'I'm going to go and get another drink,' I said, shattering the long silence. He nodded his head, gratefully.

And yes, I unashamedly love fashion and I love clothes. I snuffle and rootle my way through an antiques market, or a vintage sale, nearly every weekend. I live near Portobello market in West London and most Saturdays I'll come home crowing, with a Gucci wool blazer for just £50, a Fair Isle cardigan, or the best pair of knee-high black leather boots I've ever owned. The way I look is a big part of me although I am not necessarily vain. The thought of losing my suitcase while on holiday appals me. I care about my own surface – that much is undeniable. But I firmly believe there's nothing wrong with that. It isn't silly, or trivial, or anti-feminist, or shameful. Sure, pandering to the surface, particularly the locus of your own body, can of course be dangerous. We all know that. We worry for Generation Z, altering their own image with free apps. Navel-gazing led Narcissus to his death, but taking pride in your surface is not the same as obsessing. One does not inevitably slide into the other.

Over and over we are taught that beauty is only skin deep. But that is not quite correct. Whether you are ill – your surface dull, creased and parched – or in peak health, what happens on the surface reverberates right through to your emotional core. Ironing out the superficial creases is an attempt to straighten out the kinks of fear, buried deep. 'When you get really ill,' said my sister, 'there's suddenly all this stuff you need' – Gaviscon, steroids, anti-nausea pills. But don't ever forget about the stuff that you *don't* need. For that is where you might find your most powerful salvation.

TAKING PRIDE IN YOUR SURFACE IS NOT THE SAME AS OBSESSING.

ROMOLA GARAI

LIFE LESSON NO.20
DON'T BE AFRAID TO BE UNPOPULAR

I've been thinking about unpopularity a lot recently, and I've been thinking about feminism. Increasingly, I feel like the only way to know if you're dedicated to a cause is if you're sacrificing something for it. You have to be willing to give something up in order to know that you're actually committed and invested in creating change. And if the only thing you're getting out of being a feminist is praise and admiration, then you're not really doing anything, are you? You're not risking anything to make a difference.

And for me, the thing that I've had to learn to get used to – but that I've found quite difficult to embrace – is speaking up when I disagree with something, even if it makes me unpopular.

It's hardest at work. Saying, 'I don't care', doesn't come naturally to me. 'I don't care if you don't like me'; 'I don't care if you think I'm being a diva'; 'I don't care if this costs me my job'. But I'm trying to get better at it, and say it anyway to directors, and producers, and writers, and hair and make-up artists. Because I think the industry that I work in has a particularly bad relationship with women, and I don't think that's changing any time soon. So unless I speak up about the things that I know are wrong – even if it makes everyone else in the room roll their eyes and say 'ugh, come *on*' – then I'll be complicit in the inequality that pervades our whole world. I'll be another weapon that's used to denigrate women, and I'm not OK with that. I'm not going to be nice or compromise just because I'm expected to. At least, I'm not going to be any more.

In *The Hour* I think it was the costuming that posed the real problem for me – I felt like I was made to look very . . . decorative. And that was something I struggled with at the time, and it's something I still really struggle with today: the idea that TV shows and films are sold on their actresses' appearances. I've lost track of the times that I've been sat on set and found myself having the most extraordinary conversations with the people in hair and make-up. 'What are we going to do about your spots?' is always a favourite. Like, why do you have to do anything about my spots? But when I was younger, they used to make me take medication so strong that it had to be prescribed by a doctor, because the idea of having a woman on screen with a less than flawless complexion was so abhorrent, there was no way that it could be allowed to happen. But the resultant unpopularity of saying 'I'm not OK with that' is still something that weighs me down. It's still something to overcome.

And that's something which I think applies to most of us. Girls are raised to value popularity. The books we read as teenagers are about characters having lots of friends – girls navigating their way to the centre of their school's social circle – and their storylines show the protagonists prioritizing their popularity above all else. I'm not saying friendship isn't important, but popularity doesn't equal friendship. And success isn't the same as being liked.

But that's not to say unpopularity can't cut you to the core. I'm always fascinated when I hear people saying, 'I was so unpopular at school', because people who were truly unpopular at school rarely advertise that fact. Being unpopular at school is such a horrible feeling – and understandably so; we're social creatures who want to belong to social groups, probably no more so than at school. But as we get older, we need to learn that quality is more important than quantity, and that true friendships are about being able to deal with disagreements, and not about sustaining average levels of equanimity. In real life, significant and important relationships are the ones where you can speak your mind and be truthful and true to yourself. The best people will always stick with you despite your honesty. And I don't think girls are taught that enough.

Obviously it all ties in to social media, and I think social media is so fucking poisonous I don't even know if I want to start getting into it. I mean, what has *happened* to us, as a society? The whole thing is like a science-fiction novel gone wrong. The fact that we're now literally looking at little screens where something pops up and tells you how many times a day someone has liked you. And we're actually using that word: *liked*. So, when we're pulling popularity apart, what does it even mean when someone 'likes' you any more? Really, it means nothing at all. But for women, it feels particularly damaging, because it plays into everything we've already been taught: that our ultimate goal in life should be to be liked. I mean, just look at the way we use the word 'diva' to contain women and stop them asking for what they want. It's used so aggressively against us, but it's never applied to a man. Mariah Carey is a brilliant artist who has sold millions and millions of records, but how dare she want some sparkling water in her dressing room? Meanwhile allegations of rape and domestic violence hover around certain male stars for years and yet they're still revered as hot property and lavished with respect by many.

I guess that the hardest thing I've had to get my head around since starting to speak my mind, is the fact that not all women are feminists and not all men are misogynists. I've met so many women in the industry who have attempted to control and limit me – just as I've worked with men who have really embraced my feminism and wanted to question gender and engage in conversations about it. You can't predict who will like you, and who won't. It makes sense, but it's tough sometimes.

Naturally I wonder how different my career might be if I played the game even more and prioritized my professional popularity. I'm lazy too, so I can't put everything down to the fact that I deliberately take a strong feminist stance about the films I make and the roles I take on! There are definitely people who wouldn't work with me again – there's no question about that – but then, there are people I wouldn't work with again either . . .

Of course, it's a bit fucking rich for me to complain, because there comes a point during filming – if you've filmed half a movie and can't be replaced, for example – when it becomes pretty hard for someone to fire you. It's not like I'm in an office. I have a lot more power, even at the level that I'm at, than a lot of women do for the whole of their working lives. So when I speak my mind, I haven't got as much to lose. But I still think it's important to try – on whatever level you can – to speak up, and face the consequences. To ignore the voice in your head that says 'mmm, maybe I won't raise that because it might make me a bit unpopular', and just say it anyway. See what happens. It could just kickstart the change you've been longing for . . .

THE BEST PEOPLE WILL ALWAYS STICK WITH YOU DESPITE YOUR HONESTY. AND I DON'T THINK GIRLS ARE TAUGHT THAT ENOUGH.

BELLA YOUNGER

LIFE LESSON NO.21
WHAT YOU ONLY KNOW IF YOU'VE HAD A NERVOUS BREAKDOWN

In March 2016 I was riding high. My Instagram account, Deliciously Stella, had just gone viral, the ink was drying on my freshly signed book deal and I was about to go on holiday to Spain with ten of my best friends.

Although I didn't know it at the time, I was also about to go through my first nervous breakdown. I'd suffered from depression and anxiety on and off since my teens and had tried a number of antidepressants to combat it. Unfortunately, my body doesn't take well to the side effects, and a combination of teeth-grinding, intense headaches and an inability to orgasm meant that as soon as I started seeing someone, the pills would end up in the bin.

Before the breakdown I'd been feeling fragile. I thought a holiday would get me back on track, but instead it triggered a spiral that lasted over a year and saw me battle the most severe depression of my life. Two days after landing in Spain I flew home, was misdiagnosed with bipolar, put on mind-numbing antipsychotics and, later, spent a month in hospital. Yet throughout that time I published a book, wrote and performed a month-long, sell-out comedy show and built an online brand. Would I advise someone else to carry on regardless too? I'm not so sure. But eighteen months since I was gently escorted on to a plane in Málaga airport, my medication is stable and I feel better and more confident in myself than ever. This is what I've learned.

Look out for warning signs – they're there for a reason

The first thing I'll say is that there's often no smoke without fire. Before I departed for Spain, I had been signed off work from my job developing comedy TV shows due to some erratic behaviour. Among other things, I had listened to Beyoncé's *Runnin'* 279 times on repeat, aggressively fake-tanned one toe, leaving the rest of my body pasty white, and had sent my boss a rather long, detailed email about roads. But as someone who's prone to melodrama, I convinced myself that I was probably over-reacting when I considered calling my psychiatrist. I was probably tired. Maybe it was just stress. After all, I did once convince myself I had meningitis after a particularly nasty hangover. Luckily my boss thought differently and he told me to take a few days off and try and get hold of a doctor. If something doesn't feel right, talk to someone and make sure you tell them everything. If I'd told my psychiatrist about that toe I might have saved myself a lot of trauma.

Whatever support network you have will be invaluable. Remember to use it

Nobody blows smoke up your arse quite like when you're feeling sad or suddenly find yourself a little bit famous. Both happened to me at the same time, so believe me, I know. But in truth, I was living a double life. On the one hand, I was an up-and-coming internet sensation, my Instagram account had 'gone viral' and my agent's phone was ringing off the hook. On the other hand, I was twenty-eight and living back home with my parents, recovering from my breakdown. The press were telling me that I was hilarious and brilliant. My family reminded me that I was kind and loved. Yet I was adjusting to new diagnoses and drugs that would completely alter my personality for the next twelve months. I felt neither hilarious nor brilliant – and sometimes still don't. But if everybody is telling you that you're wonderful, and you're never quite believing it, it's perhaps time to ask yourself why. I know now that the illness was eating away at my self-esteem. And while I might not be kind, brilliant or hilarious all the time, I can see now that I am always loved, and that's always important to remember.

You will find safety in shared experience

In the lead-up to my first hospital stay, I became obsessed with famous people who shared my diagnosis. I can tell you that Catherine Zeta-Jones and Sinead O'Connor have bipolar, but it was Sylvia Plath who was my kryptonite. At my worst, I read *The Bell Jar* every single day, prompting my mother to remind me that as we had an Aga, I wouldn't have much luck making an exit like my new-found heroine.

Laughter is the best medicine

There is nothing on earth that cannot be joked about. See above. Although it was the worst time of my life, I'm lucky that I never struggle to see pockets of light in a terrible situation. It's never good to be glib of course, but laughing at something is a brilliant way of making it less terrifying. When I was at the Priory, the hospital hired a cardboard cut-out of the Queen for her jubilee, which tickled me hugely. It is possible to be happy and depressed. Enjoy those moments when you can.

People are ready to help if you're willing to ask

When people you love are struggling with their mental health, it's often difficult to know how to help. I quickly learned that if you tell people what you need, they will probably do their best to help you get it. When I decided to leave Spain and fly home to my parents' house to recuperate, I realized there was one thing standing in my way – my job. I called my father in hysterical tears from Málaga airport and begged him for his help. He called my boss the very next day and resigned on my behalf. At the time he was on holiday with my mum to celebrate their twenty-fifth wedding anniversary. My mum was just as brilliant, coaxing me out of the darkest times of my life, while also finding time to take pictures of me with crunchies strapped to my abs. You'll be amazed at how willing people are to help, if you tell them what you need.

If at first you don't succeed, try, try again

Not all therapists are created equal. Finding the right one is a lot like dating: you've got to meet a few before you settle down. Some will make you uncomfortable by telling you that you're pretty all the time, and some you will have to ghost because you don't know how to consciously uncouple. If anyone compares you to Princess Diana, run like the wind. This happened to me once and I've never forgotten it.

There isn't always 'no time like the present'

Don't be afraid to press pause on opportunities. You haven't really 'only got one shot'. Everyone experiences burnout, and when burnout leads to breakdowns this is an important rule to heed. When I was very ill, I was also very in demand in my career. I would leave the hospital on day release to attend meetings with production companies, convinced that if I missed them I would never get the TV career I craved. One producer told me to remember to take it easy, 'otherwise you might end up in a mental hospital,' he joked. I had my Priory slippers in my rucksack. Of course I should have stopped taking meetings immediately and focused on getting better, but I didn't. I accepted all offers with alacrity and hugely delayed my recovery. I will never make this mistake again. Should I have done a month-long run at the Edinburgh Festival immediately after coming out of hospital? Probably not. Would it have mattered if I'd done the show this year instead? Definitely not. Learning to say no will become your strongest asset.

Success will not immunize you from pain

I used to think that the validation of success, acclaim and even fame would ensure that I felt wonderful for ever. I used to look at famous people and fantasize about their perfect lives. Life's got to be great when you're perpetually on the beach, right? Inwardly feeling my worst when outwardly I've been doing my best has taught me that everything isn't always as it seems. My Instagram has often told a different story to the one behind the filter, and so has everyone else's.

Talking about yourself will not cover up how you're feeling inside

One of my favourite distraction techniques when I started to feel low was to deliver monologues about how well I was doing to the nearest available listener. I've never been a wallflower and couldn't bear the thought of people thinking I was shy. In my mind this made me seem fun and interesting. In reality I came across as selfish and boring. Nobody cares that you've been asked to be the face of a haircare brand. Talking about work is boring, and in this instance also confusing, because my hair is a bit crap. It would have been much better to admit that I was feeling rubbish and leave it at that.

All experience is relative

When I was in hospital I would sit in group therapy and we would be asked the reason for our being there. I would always shudder with embarrassment when it came to my turn. While some cited grief and marriage breakdowns, I had to admit that I just had too many Instagram followers and I wasn't quite sure what to do. Whatever your reason for being there, it's your reason and it still matters.

SUSAN RILEY

LIFE LESSON NO.22
NEVER MAKE ASSUMPTIONS ABOUT ANYONE

I do not like tea or coffee. Never have. Never will. It's not a health thing; I just don't like the taste of either. This is such a small, insignificant thing for me, but to others it can be quite a big deal.

Ooh they say: DON'T YOU? So what DO you drink? Do you like any hot drinks at all?

Sometimes I feel like quite the specimen.

To the extent that I apologize for my lack of 'normality': I'm sorry, I say. I'm one of those very weird people who don't like either of those things. Pass me by. Don't mind me.

Because it's only once you stand on the periphery of hot-drink culture that you realize that tea or coffee is the crux of everything. The common denominator in a room full of strangers; an expression of care and sympathy; something to do when you're bored and need to occupy your hands. It is a daily ritual. For many, a fix; the absolute first thing they do when they get up in the morning and possibly – in its most relaxing incarnation – the last thing they do before going to bed at night. So if you're just not that into either? Well, it's a lonely place to be.

I'd even say it makes people a little uncomfortable. At work functions I'll get batted towards a jug of water (YUM – a real treat) and when friends put the kettle on, I abstain from refreshments altogether so as not to cause a scene. Either way, it is a pretty depressing experience. Not as depressing as the time my brother once served me a glass of cold tea and told me it was Coca-Cola so as to really test my mettle, but depressing all the same. I just don't ever seem to be catered for.

The reason this irks me is the whole taken for granted nature of it all. Tea OR coffee. You surely must like one. It is assumed; making it in my mind a fitting metaphor for so many more things in life.

Because while I realize Earl Greys and espressos sit at the more trivial end of the scale, there are countless other assumptions made every day; the beverage question replicated a million times over whenever people don't fit in with the perceived norm. These wider suppositions cover everything from education and background to sexuality and marital status. Where did you go to university? A terribly presumptive and alienating question when directed at anyone who hasn't worn a mortarboard. What does your husband do? The subconscious expectation that any woman wearing a wedding band has a he at home as opposed to a she. Why aren't you drinking? An enquiry that might as well be phrased 'what's wrong with you?' as we invariably decide said sober person is either an incredible dullard or pregnant. And on it goes. Daily conversational chitchat is loaded with assumption: it by no means caters for all.

Don't get me wrong, I've asked these same questions countless times – they are harmless and well intentioned – but as time passes I'm really trying to change the way I ask them. Mainly so that, if the person I'm asking them of isn't able to offer a stock response, they don't end up feeling more ostracized or apologetic than they need to.

If I'm honest I think these semantics only dawn on you fully once you've had to veer away from stock responses yourself. Which can sometimes mean either something wonderful has happened to you ('What do I do? Why, nothing at all! I won £10 million on the lottery'), or something truly shit and life changing has occurred. This latter option can mean that no, not all people who don't drink are doing a triathlon or completing Dry January; some of them are recovering alcoholics who've been to the brink and back. We all know more of these people than we think we do. Be kind to them.

For me my stock answers run dry when people ask where my parents live, or if I'm seeing them at Christmas, and then I have to tell them that nowhere and no I'm not; that I'm terribly sorry but I don't have parents any more. This solemn newsflash is something I've been relaying to new colleagues and acquaintances now for fourteen years and yet – even though there's something altogether less dramatic about being an adult orphan at forty as opposed to twenty-six – I still find the assumption that I have a mum and a dad terribly alienating. And remember, we already know I don't drink tea or coffee so I'm on the fringes as it is.

Because family – precisely like that warm, comforting cuppa – is also the crux of everything. And for me there seems to be an expected ideal of one; that in order to be desirable and coveted, a family has to be large and jovial and bursting at the seams. So if you don't have that, and yours has shrunk to virtual nothingness, it's like people don't know how to entertain you.

I am of course not suggesting that we go round walking on eggshells, delicately pussyfooting around every enquiry in case we get an uncomfortable silence or shocking revelation. But I do think we'd benefit from more consideration of each other's situations, experiences and histories when we do connect, remaining open to the possibility – no, *probability* – that someone else's reality is very different to our own.

For example, I am never asked: Do you still have family? Or, What family do you have? I am asked about my parents as if they are an established fact, which I then have the responsibility to make false. The whole set up is like a recurring bad gag followed by a giant tumbleweed and stumbled apology before we swiftly move on. (BTW, please, PLEASE don't move on. If someone ever tells you their parents – or anyone for that matter – are dead, unless it's recent and they'd rather not talk about it for fear of exploding with snot and tears, just ask them something, ANYTHING about them. What were they called? What telly did they watch on a Sunday? Who does he/she most take after? Something that allows the orphaned among us to feel like part of the norm for that split second and remember that no, they weren't figments of our imagination; they were real and they were ours, if only for a shorter time than most.)

Of course, the biggest assumption we make is reserved not for the generation above, but the one below: children. Societally we remain phenomenally bad at catering for those who don't want to entertain the concept of having a family – specifically women. It's still woefully assumed that a woman isn't complete until she's found her happy-ever-after in the form of marriage and kids. The single or child-free woman is presumed unhappy; a failure. 'Yes, that is my entire life,' a friend of mine told me. 'The fact that I am single at forty: the assumption is I must be a hard-nosed ambitious cow who has actively chosen that life; or a nightmare to go out with; or a fabulous nympho like Samantha from *Sex and the City*. I could go on.'

Her advice? Simple. Don't ask, 'Are you with someone?' Or 'Are you single?' Because there's a 50/50 chance of this exceptionally closed question making someone feel sidelined.

Other gems to steer clear of: Do you want kids? (avoid, avoid – never assume someone is willing or able). Are you sure you don't want kids? (there is nothing worse than people assuming you will change your mind eventually). And my personal favourite: Are you having another? Which, as a mummy of one, I get asked ALL the time. I have no idea why we assume one isn't enough. Why isn't it? Since when can't a small family be a complete family? Do we have to push the Waltons out of our vaginas before people seem happy we're done?

There are not enough words in this book to go through all of the assumptions we make about others and what we perceive to be 'normal'. And I hasten to add the few I have listed here are merely ones from my own perspective: that of a working-class, heterosexual, able-bodied, white woman. They are the tip of the iceberg. I can only imagine the scores that a diverse collective of us could come up with between us.

Recalibrating what we consider normal or standard can take time and effort, but is straightforward to do. Life experience and empathy help. The more unexpected twists and turns my life has taken the better I become at checking my assumptions at the door. It's all a bit like one of those 'choose your own adventure' books; there are so many more narratives to encounter than we initially think there are.

But the main thing to conquer is language; the most powerful tool in the world. As a journalist and editor, I have always known the power of the written word, but I've discovered the spoken word needs just as much crafting and editing. And so I edit: Where's home? Do you have family there still? What's your partner called? How long have you not drunk for? Said out loud, language has the power to either draw someone in or push them out; it lets others feel like their normal *is* normal.

And so my life lesson remains this: assume nothing. Rephrase closed questions. Be open to every answer and scenario; know how to cater for the reply. And, most importantly, don't expect everyone to drink tea or coffee. Hot chocolate though? Well that's a different story . . .

RENI
EDDO-LODGE

LIFE LESSON NO.23
**THE POWER OF
SAYING 'NO'**

You have as many hours in the day as Beyoncé, or so proclaims the infamous meme. And it strikes a chord. After all, who *wouldn't* want to achieve the superhuman productivity of Beyoncé? A viral quote that compares you, an ordinary woman juggling life's demands, and Beyoncé's largely unattainable achievements, is a commentary on how you use your time.

I know that when I first saw it, it made me evaluate my everyday actions – and it made me feel like I was doing something wrong. It took years for me to learn that my productivity problems weren't because I was being lazy, or not Knowles-enough. They were because my priorities were all wrong. 'Prioritize like Beyoncé', the meme should say. 'Say "no" like Beyoncé.' Because unlike seconds, minutes and hours, priorities are harder to measure. But they dictate how we each use our time. And if you don't get a grip on your own quickly, then everyone else will.

At the time of writing this essay, I'm a month away from the publication of my very first book. By some fluke of fortune, I'm also in the amazing, unlikely, mind-breaking position of dealing with a huge amount of interest in it. This is very unusual for a first-time author – so much so, that the received wisdom is just to be grateful for what little coverage you get. I have the luxury of choice – which means navigating the interest of four magazines with huge circulations, two major broadcasters, three established online publishers and four podcasts. There are plans for an excerpt of my book in print, and I'll be spending a total of a month on a book tour, both in the UK and abroad.

I am overwhelmed with all the work I need to complete in the next month. This is an amazing problem to have. I'm under no illusion that this is the norm, and that I shouldn't get used to this level of interest. I know people who've had to pay for their own book tour because their publisher didn't care to publicly push their work to the press. In the attention economy, I am winning. In a month, for better or worse, my face will be splashed everywhere.

But I can't do it all. I'm just one woman, with one body and one brain (and a very good and diligent publicist) and my plate is too full. My life is consumed by low-level anxiety, and the book's not even out yet. So I've written a list of everything I've been asked to do, and I'm choosing to turn things down. I will be saying 'no' to some amazing opportunities, but I have to prioritize the things I commit myself to. Otherwise I will overstretch myself, and do everything badly.

I WILL BE SAYING 'NO' TO SOME AMAZING OPPORTUNITIES, BUT I HAVE TO PRIORITIZE THE THINGS I COMMIT MYSELF TO.

I'm trying to extend this philosophy to the other areas of my life. Before I was an author I was (and still am) a freelance writer, a job at the sharp end of the saying 'time is money'. Constantly juggling short- and long-term deadlines, I was often pushed to react to other people's needs instead of being proactive about my own. Writing about race, I would interact regularly with editors and producers who wanted me to contribute to their sensationalism, like a TV debate about the nuances of racism with someone who doesn't believe that racism exists. Once I realized the futility of these situations, I decided to set my own agenda. That's why I wrote a book. Once I knew where I wanted to go in my life – what I wanted to do – it was easier to say 'no' to things that wouldn't get me there. I said 'no' to silly requests. It meant I earned a lot less money, but I was more focused, and happier.

Of course, it's easier to say 'no' to people you don't really know than to those you care about deeply. It's all very well prioritizing our own wants and aspirations, but we still have to contend with the time we owe to others. Before, I struggled to keep up with my obligations to other people. I bailed at the last minute, and forgot my promises. Now I fiercely protect that time and those commitments. Romantic or platonic – our support networks need constant nourishment, and it's an important part of being an emotionally intelligent adult.

Yet when I click on the Facebook profiles of old acquaintances or former colleagues, I read bios that specify that these young women are currently 'wives, mothers, daughters, sisters and friends'. These descriptions suggest to me that they see themselves primarily through their relationships with other people – and I can't help but see more obligations. Don't get me wrong, I hope I am good at being all of those things on that list, but I don't think I can do any of those things well without putting my own personal growth first.

As women, we're expected to self-sacrifice. Our passions are expected to be in complete alignment with the goals and aims of our loved ones. Their achievements are our achievements. I guess it makes sense: we were never supposed to be here, out in the world, participating in public life. Women have traditionally been providing the relief and support for men to achieve their dreams. We provided the relief by looking pretty, and we provided support by ironing their clothes and making their food, keeping their houses clean and raising their children. And we were taught that this was our natural calling, and that we should like it. But second-wave feminism shattered those notions, and now women are out in the world. It's taken a century – a very short amount of time in the grand scheme of things – for us to attain an education, find jobs and travel freely. But even though we're out of the home and into the public sphere, there's still this expectation that we must bend over backwards to accommodate everyone else – to put our own priorities on the back burner – just because.

We all have our obligations in life, but we're allowed to reassess them. I think feminism will have won when every single woman feels zero discomfort about relentlessly prioritizing her own needs and goals. These needs and goals will be different for every woman, and not necessarily anchored to her family *or* her career. For me, I needed to get my book out of my brain and onto a wad of paper, so I spent the best part of a decade doing so. People might not understand why you're doing it, but you've got to carry on regardless. You've got to learn to say 'no'. You owe it to the most important person in the world: you.

12 WAYS TO SAY 'NO'

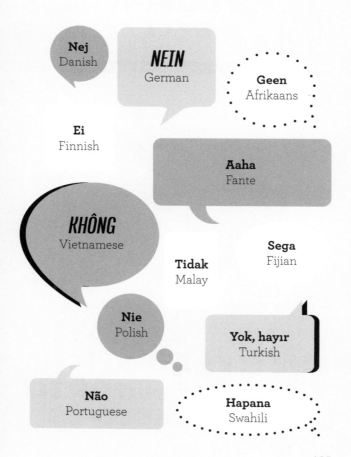

Nej
Danish

NEIN
German

Geen
Afrikaans

Ei
Finnish

Aaha
Fante

KHÔNG
Vietnamese

Sega
Fijian

Tidak
Malay

Nie
Polish

Yok, hayır
Turkish

Não
Portuguese

Hapana
Swahili

POORNA BELL

LIFE LESSON NO.24

THE FIVE QUESTIONS EVERYONE NEEDS TO ASK THEMSELVES

I am curled up on the couch watching a cheesy film. It's the kind of day that lends itself to film watching: rain gusting outside, the wind pressing its fingernails in the cracks of windows, the sky a bruise of blue and grey.

In this film, a woman finds out she only has a few weeks left to live. She sells everything she owns, and spends it all on the trip of a lifetime. (Of course, it turns out she isn't dying at all, but hey-ho.)

A few years ago, when my life was solely about social plans for the weekend and making a success of my career, I wouldn't have given this movie a second thought after the end credits rolled.

But now I find myself asking so many questions – perhaps the most important of which is: why does it take something as extreme as death to ignite the courage to live the life you want?

It takes some people entire lifetimes to work out what they really want. Some people never get there at all. And some, like me, arrive at it through the hardest route imaginable – as the result of immense loss.

Two years ago, my husband Rob passed away by suicide. When Rob was alive, he taught me a lot about love. How it felt to be loved unconditionally and so immensely. But he also taught me how complicated life really was. He had been struggling with chronic depression since he was a child, and developed a formidable heroin addiction as a means – I believe – to self-medicate it.

Two days after Rob died, I found myself in the funeral home. This was the first time I was to see his body. I entered a small room, and saw him lying there, still, so still, and I remember how tightly my mind coiled away from the reality I had now found myself in.

It was him, and yet it wasn't. I had never, in all the kisses we had shared, ever seen his mouth attain that tinge of blue. And I realized, just before the ground cracked beneath my feet to swallow me in grief, the true finality of death. There is no bargaining, and no amount of begging that will permit the universe to turn the clock back.

In the months that followed, I realized the only way of surviving the experience of him dying was to understand I was no longer the same person. For a long time, I felt like I had one foot in the world of the dead, and one foot in the land of the living. And when I was finally able to actively embrace being in the latter, I realized I had to ask some serious questions about my life.

Questions I had never thought to ask myself before because the irony of life, of course, is that it takes something as uncompromising as death to figure out what really counts.

My life these days is far from perfect, but it is more honest.

The hard truth is that we are all going to die. We may never know how or when; the only guarantee is that we will. Yet we live our lives as if we have an endless supply of time, of second chances, as if this is the rehearsal when it is the performance.

I may hold more sadness than I used to, but I understand what makes me content and happy. I have no space for regret or bitterness. These are the questions I asked myself in order to get here . . .

Question One:
What do you want to be remembered for?

'I'm really glad I worked those extra hours/sat in loads of meetings/ate lunch at my desk every day,' said no one on their deathbed ever. If you can ask yourself this question and answer truthfully, it will reveal a fragile compass of sorts, guiding you towards what you want.

As much as I love my job as a senior woman in business, I don't want people to remember I was a great manager. Or that I hit my targets. All of the sleepless nights and sacrifices I make on behalf of work are not going to amount to anything I want to be said about me in a eulogy.

Asking myself this question forced a sense of clarity, at a time when I was feeling under pressure at work. As I walked the block around our office, my eyes puffy with crying from stress, I thought: 'Does this actually matter? In two months, or even a year's time, will anyone actually remember this thing you're worried about?' And that made me think: 'Well, what do I actually want to be remembered for?'

I realized I wanted to be a good aunt, a loving sister. I wanted to spend proper time with my parents, not treat them like an afterthought.

And I wanted my legacy to be my writing – the reason why I got into journalism in the first place. I couldn't do anything about Rob being dead, but I could somehow use my writing to fashion my grief into a tool that helped me and other people. I ended up turning all of my catharsis into a book about mental health and humanity.

Realigning my work gave me a renewed sense of purpose because for once I wasn't just trying to get through the week. I wanted each day to count for something.

Question Two:
Who are you comparing yourself to?

Most of us are in the same echo chamber.

It consists of career and money one-upmanship. Have you bought a house? Are you married? Do you have kids? We spin these stories around dinner tables, over drinks and at work, until we yearn for something we may not even want.

When Rob died, I found myself in a pretty small club: young widows and widowers. Society, frankly, doesn't know what to do with us. It can't fool us that marriage is the path to happiness, it can't push us into having children when that no longer is an option (at least not for a long time).

I spent a while after his death feeling angry – uncontrollable swirls of bitterness and rage – because life hadn't turned out like I wanted it to. Because my friends were married and having kids, and I knew I was nowhere near ready. I felt like life was relentlessly moving on, and I was pinned by my grief.

But you know what? I started thinking about what Rob had given me. He made me feel beautiful, he restored my self-esteem, and his profound respect for women set the baseline of how I wanted to be treated when I was ready to enter into a relationship.

I also examined whether I really wanted children. The answer: ambivalent.

What I realized, is that being in the echo chamber makes it really hard to distinguish your personal goals from everyone else's expectations. So I asked myself whose life was I comparing myself to? And did I want to be like them?

Spoiler: I did not.

Question Three:
Why the fuck are you saying 'yes' to everything?

When Rob and I were trying to manage his depression and addiction, we went to great pains to present a front to the world, that everything was fine and we were like any other normal couple.

Maintaining this fake life while trying to battle two of the most formidable mental health issues was exhausting. We went to first birthdays, baby showers, barbecues. We said 'yes' to weddings even though we could barely afford rent, let alone the bride and groom's present. We said 'yes' because we felt saying 'no' would arouse too much suspicion, and people would think we were bad friends.

Death is like turpentine; it strips away artifice to reveal what is really underneath because you don't have the energy to maintain a façade.

What I came to realize is that everyone, in their own way, says 'no' to things, especially if it doesn't suit them, or if it's inconvenient. And when I realized this, I wanted to kick myself for the number of times I had said 'yes', when we just didn't have the space or energy for it.

If you say 'no', people won't hate you. It may be a blow to the ego but in time, they probably won't even remember.

But the amount of oxygen you create in your life by saying 'no' a bit more can be life-changing. So if you feel stretched, burdened and are so over-booked you can only make plans with a three-month lead time, it's time to ask yourself what you're actually getting out of this.

Question Four:
Where do you really want to be this time next year?

I was sitting in my therapist's office, and I was in the middle of a diatribe about how unhappy I was with my life. 'Everyone's moving on, no one gives a shit, I should just leave and go live in a hermit shack.'
'Well what would you do in this shack?' she asked.

I didn't know where to begin – my head was a jumble of thoughts but that's fairly normal with grief – sometimes the pieces of you are scattered so wide it's hard to pull together linear thought.

Seeing how I was struggling, she asked me to think about my life, and said: 'If everything is exactly the same in a year's time, would you be alright with that?'

Vehemently, I was not. The minute I started to visualize what life would be like, I couldn't breathe. I felt trapped; it seemed inconceivable that I would be doing exactly the same thing in twelve months' time. In that moment, although I didn't quite know what the future was going to look like, I knew exactly what had to change, and that started the process of figuring it out.

We usually make these lists on New Year's Day as an absolution from the broken promises of the previous year. We think about the things we've always wanted to experience or become. While these lists are worthwhile, they also end up being a distraction from what we're really unhappy about. Some of them become a form of escapism.

By asking me to look at my life and to imagine the future exactly as it was in the present, my therapist gently made me confront what I was really unhappy about. Because until I knew that, I would always seek the solution to my misery in something else, when really, the answer was much closer than I realized.

Question Five:
What kind of person do you want to be?

Unless you are Madonna you don't often get the chance to redefine yourself. The main reason being: re-forming into a different person is an incredibly hard and painful process. You have to truly face the things that give you most pain, shame and sadness. It is often too hard to look at.

If you had known me five years ago, you might think I'm the same person now. I still throw my head back when I laugh, and I still snigger when Cockfosters comes up on the Piccadilly line. But I know the arrangement of myself is different.

Trauma forces change upon you. You have no option because the person you were before the trauma no longer exists – the intensity of experience has burned you beyond recognition.

When Rob died, there were parts of him that were magnificent. He was always so much kinder than I was. Less judgmental. Hugely empathetic, he would put himself out to help anyone.

I held onto the things my husband loved about me (even if I didn't see them myself). I wanted to become kinder and help people; so I did, just by asking: what would Rob do?

But that doesn't mean you can't change in the absence of trauma. That you can't look at the aspects of your life – identify what you don't like – and make an attempt to alter it.

Real, substantial change takes time, and it is the result of a hundred different, tiny decisions you make about your life. But it is possible – if you are willing to be brave enough. And it means that you end up becoming a person you like and respect, rather than seeking that validation from other people.

FRANCESCA MARTINEZ

LIFE LESSON NO.25
GIVE NORMALITY A KICK IN THE ARSE

When I was a kid, I felt normal. Of course, I knew that certain things like walking, writing and doing up buttons were harder for me, but that was just the way things were. Occasionally, at school, my eyes would flick across to a classmate and admire the remarkably non-wobbly letters that flowed gracefully from her hand, before my gaze returned to puzzle at my own exercise book, littered as it was with erratic shapes that vaguely resembled the alphabet. Or some kind of alphabet. If you squinted. And when we played tag at break-times, I was well aware that I could never escape the clutches of my friends, no matter how hard I tried to run. This was simply my reality. I was Francesca. And Francesca had curly hair, two big front teeth and was wobbly.

The words 'cerebral palsy' haunted me like an unwanted ghost, but most of the time I was pretty successful at making it disappear. Like most kids, I had far more important things to worry about than how my brain functioned or how much coordination I had. There were trees to climb, boys to fall in love with and my grandma's apple pie to devour. I didn't know it at the time, but my young parents had been given a typically negative framing of my condition when I was diagnosed at two years old. The medical community seems to regard disability as a tragic mistake, a cruel aberration of nature. They transmit this unhelpful attitude to most parents, delivering it with suitably solemn words, grave faces, ugly labels and pessimistic prognoses of the wretched futures that await their beloved kids. Fortunately my parents realized that the consultant was talking through his white-coated arse, and decided there and then that they would just love me as their child. I can't thank them enough for having had the strength to be positive in that moment. I'm sure it's been the decisive factor in shaping me into the person I am today. Add to them a pair of Spanish grandparents who were – frankly, insanely – devoted to their wobbly granddaughter, and my home was an idyllic place to be. Yes, there were arguments and tantrums (I was normal, remember), but I was a confident, happy tomboy who loved life, had a cheeky sense of humour and a lust for performing. I felt as far away from abnormal as you could possibly be.

Then I went to high school. And not just any high school. An all-girls one. Within a month, my self-worth had evaporated and the confidence that had shone through me was reduced to the barest flicker of a flame. You could say it was a wake-up call. And a rather shrill one at that.

I realized with a jolt that the world around me viewed me as different, abnormal – disabled. For the first time in my life, I became aware of a huge disconnect between how I saw myself and how others saw me. I tried in vain to make friends, to be funny, to win people over with my generosity. But all that mattered, apparently, was how I walked, how I talked and how different I was. The obvious solution to me was to try to be as 'normal' as possible. So I tried my best to walk and talk like everybody else, to avoid asking for help and to be the cheeriest person on the planet. I failed, of course. That pesky brain damage couldn't be suppressed, which was annoying. Finally I retreated into myself, kept my head down and hoped the five years would fly by.

They didn't, but there was one blessing. A pretty enormous one. I got cast in a TV show called *Grange Hill* as – you guessed it – a wobbly schoolgirl. I ended up missing nine months of school a year. For five years. Legally! The show was great fun. My confidence started to return, I had real friends (not imaginary ones) and started to enjoy life again. Then I left the show when I was eighteen and made friends with unemployment. Every day, the same thought flashed across my mind: 'I wish I was normal.' It became my mantra. I was convinced that, somehow, if I attained this prized goal, all my problems and worries would float away like untethered balloons, and I'd live happily ever after.

I never managed to become normal. Instead, I did the opposite. Hitting my own personal rock-bottom, I was forced, for my own survival, to make a change. Lying in bed one night, I decided to accept myself exactly as I was and stop trying to be anybody else. Simple. But the results were immediate and staggering. The minute I came out of the wobbly closet and accepted who I was, other people did the same. 'Normal' people. They followed my example and accepted who I was too. Of course, there was – is – still the odd (very odd, if you ask me) person who tilted their head and talked to me as if I was two, but I stopped caring about how they perceived me. I knew I had no power to control what everyone else thought of me, but I did have the power to choose what I thought of myself. And that was enough. I gained enough self-worth to start doing stand-up comedy. Which, it has to be said, is perfect for toughening you up and forcing you to be yourself – no barriers, no masks, just you. It was exactly what I needed and I took to it with a passion that bordered on obsession.

As I did more and more shows, I began to question the labels that had been plastered all over me, and how society defined me by what I *couldn't* do. I realized I didn't have to define myself by those inaccurate, ugly, reductive and misleading labels, so I dumped them all. I was Francesca and I was wobbly, but I was no more or less different than anyone else walking (or rolling) around this planet. Everyone has things they can't do. That's what is normal. We all have our struggles and challenges. It's part of being human. And in the months that followed, it turned out that nearly everyone I met was struggling to be normal, to fit in, to like themselves. Feeling abnormal – or, at least, not good enough – it seems, is totally normal after all. More importantly, I realized that I had never actually met a 'normal' person. Where were they all hiding? Finally, at twenty-one, I felt a normal part of the human race.

Still, it was a shock to learn that my battles to accept myself actually had nothing to do with being wobbly, and everything to do with living in a culture that breeds dissatisfaction and 'aspiration'. We're taught to compare ourselves to people who are richer and, apparently, more beautiful than we are, to believe that happiness comes from buying stuff. Well, that couldn't be further from the truth. When I discovered my happiness, I didn't change anything externally. I didn't buy a catwalk frock or get rat poison injected into my face. I just accepted myself, and recognized that how my body works or looks doesn't define me. And, although it's well nigh impossible to escape these unhealthy messages, I realized that we all have the power to reject them and pursue healthier, more fulfilling goals. Frankly, accepting yourself as you are is an act of civil disobedience!

So no, the biggest impact on my life hasn't been my body, but instead the love I've received and the values I've chosen to embrace. What we call 'disability', I learnt, is a natural and normal part of humanity. Suddenly I felt lucky to be alive. After all, I didn't have to exist. None of us had to. But we do, in all manner of unique and marvellous ways. How amazing is that?

6 PIONEERING FEMALE COMICS:

LUCILLE BALL

The queen of slapstick, Lucille Ball (1911–1989), did it her way.
After working across American film and radio in the 40s, CBS
offered Ball her own TV show in 1950. *I Love Lucy* became
America's most watched show (it still attracts 40 million
viewers a year thanks to syndication), spawned the sitcom
genre and was the first to be filmed in front of a live audience,
thanks to Ball's ability to play off a crowd. Ball was also the
first female CEO of a major production company.

JOAN RIVERS

Whip-smart and very, very funny, American Joan Rivers (1933–2014) made the one-liner an art form, proving comedy wasn't just for the boys. Featuring on the US's *The Tonight Show* in 1965, her career spanned six decades and in 1986 she became the first woman to have her own late-night talk show. Sex, religion, her husband's suicide and her own plastic surgery were all fair game, with her work inspiring comics as diverse as Chris Rock and Sarah Silverman.

VICTORIA WOOD

In her teens, Brit Victoria Wood (1953–2016) plotted how to become the greatest female entertainer of her day. And she did just that . . . A belly laugh-inducing stand-up, actress, singer and TV dramatist with a CBE and seven BAFTA awards to her name, in fact. Part of Wood's genius was the juxtaposition of a dry humour with northern roots, and her ability to bolster talent, including Julie Walters, Maxine Peake and Susie Blake. If in doubt, seek out the inspired 'Two Soups' sketch.

WHOOPI GOLDBERG

One of only twelve people to land an EGOT (Emmy, Grammy, Oscar and Tony), American Whoopi Goldberg (born 1955) broke out in 1984 with a dazzling one-woman show. From her serious turn in *The Color Purple* (1985) to the cheerfully bonkers million-dollar *Sister Act* films – for a while in the 90s she was the highest paid actress of all time – and her LGBT activism, she's broken down barriers across the board while remaining a Hollywood comedy stalwart.

TINA FEY

Combining dry wit with adroit pop-culture references, Fey has knocked down every hurdle in the male-dominated world of comedy, both behind and in front of the camera. After training in improv – where she met fellow comedian Amy Poehler – Fey became *Saturday Night Live*'s first head writer in 1999 – where she also famously impersonated Sarah Palin, wrote *Mean Girls* and starred as the self-deprecating, wildly witty Liz Lemon in *30 Rock*. Fey's awards cabinet – containing eight Emmys to date – is testament to her status on the contemporary comedy scene.

PHOEBE WALLER-BRIDGE

Born in 1985, British Waller-Bridge came into public consciousness like a gut punch in 2016 with her BBC3 sitcom *Fleabag* – based on her 2013 one-woman play of the same name. Her show's protagonist, Fleabag, is flawed, furious, sexual, sharp-tongued and truly funny. On screen nothing is off limits. She shows womanhood in all its messy facets, making her both refreshing and revolutionary, and garnering her huge critical acclaim on both sides of the Atlantic.

1. LISA SMOSARSKI

Lisa Smosarski is the launch editor of the award-winning women's weekly *Stylist*. Launched in September 2009, *Stylist* is the first freemium magazine for women. As editor she has seen *Stylist* win forty-one industry awards, including PPA editor of the year in 2012 and BSME launch of the year in 2010, plus overseen nine consecutive ABC rises. Prior to this, Lisa was the editor of *more!*, *bliss* and *Smash Hits*, launch edited *mykindaplace.com* and has been a contributor to many UK magazines. In 2006 Lisa also presented the Channel 4 TV series *Make Me a Grown Up*.

2. BOBBI BROWN

Bobbi Brown is an American make-up artist, entrepreneur and titan of the beauty industry. After graduating college as a theatrical make-up artist, Brown created a range of cosmetics in natural shades, designed to enhance rather than dominate a woman's beauty. She founded Bobbi Brown Cosmetics in 1991, and four years later her chic, less-is-more brand was purchased by Estée Lauder. Eventually stocked in more than seventy countries, it became one of the world's most popular make-up brands, hitting revenues of $1bn. In 2016, at the age of fifty-nine, Brown announced she was stepping down from the Chief Creative Officer's chair, to rediscover her love of creating products and to launch a new lifestyle brand.

3. LAURA JANE WILLIAMS

Laura Jane Williams writes about love, sex and being human. Starting out with a blog, 'Superlatively Rude', she shared her frank experiences of dating, porn, lust and rejection. Her intensely personal book *Becoming: Sex, Second Chances and Figuring Out Who the Hell I Am*, about going celibate after being rejected by her childhood sweetheart, was followed by *Ice Cream for Breakfast*, which chronicled her anxiety and quest for happiness. As well as writing for leading magazines, Williams – who lives in London – also runs writing workshops, gives talks on creativity and is a frequent commentator on social media.

4. NIMKO ALI

Campaigner Nimko Ali has transformed countless young girls' lives by breaking the taboo around female genital mutilation (FGM). Refugees from Somalia, Ali's family moved to the UK when she was four. At seven she was forced to undergo FGM, and in her twenties, Ali helped set up Daughters of Eve, a non-profit organization to raise awareness of the barbaric practice. Following her work, legislation was passed to protect young girls across the UK from FGM. Ali has been named on the *Woman's Hour* Power List, shaped the 'End FGM/C Social Change' campaign, written a no-holds-barred memoir *Rude: There is no such thing as over-sharing* and stood as an MP for the Women's Equality Party.

5. TANYA GOLD

Journalist and former *Stylist* columnist Tanya Gold is fearless in her political opinions and unflinching in her revelations. Diagnosed with alcoholism in her late twenties, Gold experienced rehab before discovering her talent for honest, powerful writing. In her twenty-year career, she's tackled an eclectic range of subjects for broadsheets and magazines alike, from the wearing of burkas and the aftermath of substance abuse to undercover investigations on reality TV. Along the way she was awarded Features Writer of the Year at the British Press Awards and won a Foreign Press Association award, and has established herself as a steely voice for those challenging societal tradition and prejudice.

6. CLARA AMFO

Radio presenter Clara Amfo worked her way up the ranks at KISS FM, being nominated for a Sony Radio 'Rising Star' award on the way in 2012 before joining BBC Radio 1 Xtra and eventually Radio 1 where she was only the second woman ever to host the BBC Radio 1 Chart Show. Today she presents the mid-morning slot, as well as presenting events including Glastonbury and the BRIT Awards on television. Amfo has branched out into documentaries, presenting *Deeper than Skin* about skin-bleaching and questions of identity, and *Running with Grief*, a personal project which explored the death of her father.

7. LUCY MANGAN

Award-winning *Stylist* columnist and author Lucy Mangan has been dissecting feminist issues ever since she turned her back on a legal career to write for a living. Starting out at the *Guardian* Mangan has since written four books, including *The Reluctant Bride: One Woman's Journey (Kicking and Screaming) Down the Aisle*. After joining *Stylist* as a columnist in 2011, she was awarded the PPA Columnist of the Year in 2013 for her frank, thought-provoking and often outrageous weekly observations. She says, 'I feel the shock and the privilege, every day, of being able to communicate with so many people – women especially – and discuss issues that affect us all.'

8. JO CLIFFORD

Credit Kim Ayres

One of Scotland's leading playwrights, Jo Clifford spent the first forty-nine years of her life as John: a husband, writer and father. She worked as a nurse, bus conductor and lecturer while writing over eighty plays, including *Losing Venice* and *Every One*, which have been performed around the world, and won theatrical awards, including the *Scotland on Sunday* Critics' Award and the Edinburgh Festival Fringe First. Now legally recognized as a woman, Jo Clifford wrote and produced *The Gospel According to Jesus, Queen of Heaven*, which examines what would happen were Jesus to return to earth as a transwoman. Inspired by her own transgender identity, Clifford has also set up Teatro do Mundo (Theatre of the World) to help create new value structures for modern society.

9. JESS PHILLIPS

A member of the Labour Party since her fourteenth birthday, Jess Phillips was elected as MP for Birmingham Yardley in 2015, and re-elected in 2017. In her pre-Westminster days, she worked for Women's Aid, a domestic sexual abuse charity, and served on the West Midlands Police and Crime Panel. In Parliament she has tirelessly supported feminist issues, including overturning the breastfeeding ban in the House of Commons Chamber, and has spoken out against the threats and abuse she received online as a result. In 2016 she was voted chair of the Women's Parliamentary Labour Party and her first book, *Everywoman: One Woman's Truth about Speaking the Truth,* was published a year later.

10. CHRISTINA LAMB OBE

Christina Lamb OBE is one of Britain's leading foreign correspondents. Named Young Journalist of the Year in 1988 for her frontline reports from the war in Afghanistan, Lamb has gone on to cover conflicts and disasters around the world. Chief Foreign Correspondent for the *Sunday Times,* she has won numerous awards for reporting and particularly focuses on women, highlighting the plight of the Yazidi girls taken as sex-slaves, those kidnapped by Boko Haram or held inside Libyan detention centres. She has been awarded Foreign Correspondent of the Year five times, the Prix Bayeux – Europe's top war-reporting award, an honorary fellowship at her alma mater, University College, Oxford, and an OBE. Lamb is also the bestselling author of eight titles, including *The Africa House, I Am Malala* and *The Girl from Aleppo: Nujeen's Escape from War to Freedom in a Wheelchair.*

11. ALIX FOX

Alix Fox is an award-winning journalist, broadcaster and sex educator. A former editor of alternative culture magazine *Bizarre* she began her career writing about extreme fetishes and sexual subcultures. She went on to write for mainstream publications, before presenting the *Guardian*'s real-life relationship podcast *Close Encounters* and appearing as an X-rated agony aunt on the podcast *The Modern Mann*. Named Sex Educator of the Year 2016, Fox has worked to improve sex education in schools and collaborated with brands such as Durex and Superdrug to open up discussion on sexual topics. She has worked with the mental health campaign Heads Together and delivered a TEDx talk, *Bonkers Bonking*, on the lessons she's learnt about sex.

12. ROXANE GAY

American writer and academic Roxane Gay has broadened our preconceptions of what it means to be a feminist and what it is to be a woman. Author of *Bad Feminist*, *Difficult Women* and *Hunger: A Memoir of (My) Body*, Gay passionately argues that women shouldn't have to struggle to live up to feminist ideals, and highlights the extreme discrimination experienced by minority women. Lecturing in English, she is a contributing writer for *The New York Times* and has also written for *Harper's Bazaar*, *McSweeney's*, *Virginia Quarterly Review* and many others. Her TED talk 'Confessions of a Bad Feminist' has received over one million views online.

13. HANNAH AZIEB POOL

Credit Aida Muluneh

Fashion, beauty and culture have become the backbone of Pool's career as a writer, curator and columnist. The first woman of colour to write a beauty column, 'The New Black', for a national British newspaper, Pool has also worked on the Women of the World (WOW) festival in London, been a cultural programmer at the Southbank Centre and chair of feminist pressure group UK Feminista. Adopted from an orphanage in Eritrea in 1974 by a white British couple, Pool wrote the moving memoir *My Father's Daughter* about her emotionally complex journey to find her long-lost father in Eritrea. Her most recent book is *Fashion Cities Africa*, a guide to contemporary African Fashion.

14. KATIE PIPER

Credit Dan Kennedy

Activist, author and inspirational speaker Katie Piper is a tireless campaigner for burns victims. As well as founding her charity The Katie Piper Foundation, which gives practical and emotional support to those living with scars, she's written five books and presented a number of TV shows which have been shown around the world. Despite enduring more than 100 operations to reconstruct her face, she agreed to reveal her identity in a Channel 4 documentary: *Katie: My Beautiful Face*. The show received over 3.5 million viewers and won Best Single Documentary at the 2010 BAFTA Television Awards. Piper appeared on *Stylist*'s cover in 2016.

15. NINA STIBBE

Author Nina Stibbe is best known for *Love, Nina: Despatches from Family Life*. A compilation of incisive, humorous letters written while she worked as a nanny in 1980s literary London, the book wasn't released until 2013 when, at the age of fifty, Stibbe finally achieved her first publishing contract. Her work won the Non-Fiction Book of the Year Award at the National Book Awards, was shortlisted for Waterstones Book of the Year and was adapted for a BBC television series. She subsequently published the comic novels *Man at the Helm* and *Paradise Lodge*, both shortlisted for the Bollinger Everyman Wodehouse Prize for Comic Fiction.

16. ANNA FIELDING

Anna Fielding is the associate editor (features) at *Stylist* magazine. She was the editor of *Emerald Street*, a daily lifestyle email for women, for six years, having launched the title. She has worked as a journalist for over seventeen years, starting out as a staff writer at *Mixmag*, and going on to contribute to many titles, including *The Times*, *NME* and *The Face*. Anna also set up the *Emerald Street* Literary Festival and has programmed the event for two years.

17. ROBYN WILDER

Freelance journalist Robyn Wilder is an advocate of awareness of mental health issues and the difficulties and prejudices faced by new mothers. Having suffered ongoing anxiety and depression, Wilder suffered a nervous breakdown at twenty-one. She held jobs in theatre, music and charities until she discovered her passion and talent for writing. Wilder frequently writes both frankly and poignantly on parenting issues, sharing the effects of the post-natal depression and post-traumatic stress disorder she suffered after the difficult birth of her son. In 2016 she was shortlisted for a Words by Women Award, acknowledging outstanding women in journalism.

18. NICOLA ADAMS OBE

Flyweight boxer Nicola Adams wasn't just the first woman to win an Olympic gold medal in boxing at London 2012; she was also the first woman to defend her title and win a second gold at Rio 2016. She has won Commonwealth, European and World boxing titles, received both an MBE and an OBE for services to boxing and turned professional in 2017. Adams was named the most influential LGBT individual by the *Independent* in 2012 and appeared on *Stylist*'s cover in 2016.

19. PANDORA SYKES

Pandora Sykes is a journalist and broadcaster. The former Fashion Features Editor at the *Sunday Times Style*, she now writes for *The Times*, the *Telegraph* and the *Guardian* and a range of international fashion magazines. Sykes also co-hosts *The High Low*, a pop-culture and news podcast, and regularly hosts panel debates about fashion, culture, digital media and all things to do with young women.

20. ROMOLA GARAI

British actress Romola Garai experienced both her professional breakthrough and her 'feminist epiphany' while starring in *Dirty Dancing: Havana Nights*. Feeling under pressure to portray negative body ideals, she subsequently turned her back on Hollywood. Since then she's focused on complex, transformative female roles in film and on TV, including Briony Tallis in *Atonement*, Bel Rowley in *The Hour*

and Alice Haughton in *Suffragette*. She has been nominated for two Golden Globes, a BAFTA award and has appeared on the cover of *Stylist* three times. Garai continues to speak out as a strong campaigning voice on feminist issues, including the gender pay gap and the plight of female asylum seekers.

21. BELLA YOUNGER

In 2016 Bella Younger was beginning her career as a comedian when she posted an image online parodying the clean eating, perfect living trend. It instantly struck a chord and she quickly gained over 140,000 followers on Instagram. As her fictional alter ego 'Deliciously Stella' she continued to use humour to harpoon the seemingly perfect worlds and extreme wellness regimes portrayed online, and achieved a sell-out one woman show at the Edinburgh Fringe Festival. Younger has also published a book, *Bella Younger's Deliciously Stella*, created a podcast, wrote and appeared in web sitcom *Happy Now* and established herself as one of Britain's leading online comedians.

22. SUSAN RILEY

Susan Riley is deputy editor – and three-times acting editor – of *Stylist*, a publishing phenomenon she has helped steer and grow since its ground-breaking launch in 2009. With fifteen years' experience working across leading media brands for women, she has been a judge for popular industry accolades such as the Cool Brands Awards and the Mr & Mrs Smith Travel Awards. In addition to curating *Stylist*'s award-winning travel section, Susan is a seasoned interviewer, presenter and brand consultant.

23. RENI EDDO-LODGE

Award-winning journalist Reni Eddo-Lodge gained literary and political headlines in 2017 with her first book *Why I'm No Longer Talking to White People about Race*. A challenge to white privilege and systemic racism in Britain, it gave a powerful voice to women of colour who felt excluded by feminism and society at large. A previous *Stylist* cover star, she's frequently invited to share her views on discrimination, intersectionality and feminism on TV and radio debates, and has also been named a judge for the BBC's *Woman's Hour* Power List.

24. POORNA BELL

Award-winning journalist Poorna Bell is an author and freelance senior editor. Previously executive editor and global lifestyle head of HuffPost UK, she's written for the *Guardian* and the *Telegraph*, and is a frequent commentator on mental health issues on television and online. Bell has been a judge for the First Women Awards, the British Book Awards and the Sony World Photography Awards. Her first book, *Chase the Rainbow*, explored depression, addiction, mental health and the nature of love, following her husband Rob's suicide in 2015.

25. FRANCESCA MARTINEZ

Comedian Francesca Martinez made her first major public impression as a recurring character on the TV show *Grange Hill*. She made her second when, in 2000, she became the first woman to win the *Daily Telegraph* Open Mic Award at the Edinburgh Festival. The combination of her humour and the upfront way in which she dealt with her cerebral palsy led to a successful career with many TV appearances (including *Live at the Apollo* and *Extras* opposite Kate Winslet) plus several worldwide comedy tours. In 2015 her debut book, *What the **** is normal?!*, was nominated for multiple comedy awards. Martinez is also a vocal campaigner, highlighting the inequality faced by those considered 'not normal'.